THE
INCH
PRINCIPLE

21 *Million Dollar Inches of Management*

Cover Design and Art Direction: Shawn Davies, Boomerang Design Group

This book is dedicated to my loving and supportive family
Sherri, Jennifer, Melody, Crystal and Mary.

John

■

This book is dedicated to my wife Kimberly, my best friend
and the love of my life! To Timothy, Stevie, Isaac, and Heidi
the best home team ever! Thank you for your belief in me.

Paul

Contents

Acknowledgments 9

Foreword 11

Lesson at 30,000 Feet 15

Introduction
The Inch Principle 19

Million Dollar Inch #1:
Never Let Your Style Get in the Way of Your Success 25

Million Dollar Inch #2:
Steal a Page from Someone Else's Playbook 35

Million Dollar Inch #3:
Don't Change You—Change the Way You Do Things 43

Million Dollar Inch #4:
Stop Looking for Solutions—Start Treating the Condition 49

Million Dollar Inch #5:
If It's Not an Exact Science, Play the Percentages 55

Million Dollar Inch #6:
Never Outsource Your Own Success 61

Million Dollar Inch #7:
Nothing Happens without Personal Responsibility 69

Million Dollar Inch #8:
Create a Balance of Power with Today's Workforce 75

Million Dollar Inch #9:
Graduate from a Day Care to an Adult Learning Center 83

Million Dollar Inch #10:
Tear Up the Statement and Live the Mission 89

11 MILLION DOLLAR INCH

Million Dollar Inch #11:

Make the Quickest Path to Success the Quickest Path to Success 95

12 MILLION DOLLAR INCH

Million Dollar Inch #12:

Memo to Everyone: Profit is Not a Four Letter Word 101

13 MILLION DOLLAR INCH

Million Dollar Inch #13:

Manage Expectations with the Stages of Trust & Accountability 107

14 MILLION DOLLAR INCH

Million Dollar Inch #14:

Beware of the Honor System 115

15 MILLION DOLLAR INCH

Million Dollar Inch #15:

Establish a Red Zone to Protect the Company 121

16 MILLION DOLLAR INCH

Million Dollar Inch #16:

Always Work to Bring Them Back from BOHICA 129

17 MILLION DOLLAR INCH

Million Dollar Inch #17:

Spend Quality Time with Your Quality People 135

18 MILLION DOLLAR INCH

Million Dollar Inch #18:

Encourage New People to Give Up Their Right to Fail 143

19 MILLION DOLLAR INCH

Million Dollar inch #19:

Close the Monkey Adoption Agency 151

20 MILLION DOLLAR INCH

Million Dollar Inch #20:

Name that Meeting 159

21 MILLION DOLLAR INCH

Million Dollar Inch #21:

Control the Schedule—Maximize Profits and Enjoy Life 167

Conclusion 175

Appendix:

The Cornerstones Management Institute 178

Meet the Principals of the Cornerstones Management Institute 179

Acknowledgements

Publishing a book requires more than just unique ideas and a successful track record in the subject matter. We have many people to thank as we publish *The Inch Principle*. We would like to start with the design, editing and administrative support team of Anne Austen, Gale Boyd, Tom Vangeloff, Shawn Davies, and Melody Biggs.

To our sources of inspiration: For Paul C – To Kimberly, my best friend and the love of my life; to my home team, Timothy, Stevie, Isaac, and Heidi; to my Parents, Everett and Gretel Carpenter, and brothers Kevin and Joel Carpenter; my business partner, John T. Condry, the Haynes and Young families; and above all, to the Lord Jesus Christ for the blessings he has shown and the opportunity to give him glory.

For John C, To my Parents, Dr. James A. Condry and Elizabeth D. Condry for all the positive qualities I possess; my partner Paul Carpenter for his commitment and shared vision of our mission; to my brothers, Raphael Joseph Condry and James D. Condry for their example of success; to my grandchildren, Cru, Mckay, Taysen, Londyn, and Adelyn for the joy they bring to my life; my in-laws, Wayne and Christine Larkins for their love and support; and last to my good friends Dan and Mary Bishop—Dan unexpect-edly passed away as we are releasing this book. Dan was my best friend, mentor, and advocate of the principles written in this book.

Thanks for their support go to Paul Nelson, Charlie Hauck, Sue Keyes, Bob Waks, Bob Sinton, Paul Lushin, Steve Montague, Steve Taback, John Hirth, Mark Berezow, Kevin Hallenbeck, Tom and Paula Scully, Al Strauss, Mark and Diane Fitzgerald, Brian McConnell, Lucius Stone, Dan Kiley, Matt Baker, Donnie Williams, Mike Knight, Steve Hand, Scott Chakan, Bob Lisser, Dave Kurlan and Tom Schaff.

We have been extremely fortunate to have clients who have made a substantial commitment to improving their management skills. We salute each of our clients for their faith and application of the principles found in this book.

And we thank you, whether you are a new friend or someone with us since the start, for your desire to grow with us.

Foreword

Two roads diverged in a wood, and I—I took the one less traveled by, and that has made all the difference.

- Robert Frost

Foreword

C an a book really be worth a million dollars? Put in the right context and applied by the right person, our track record responds with a resounding YES! The right context is the application across an organization, and the right person is you.

As members of the on-demand generation, we have become impatient. Look around you; there's a "fast, quick, instant, speedy, easy, or guaranteed" fad, tool, book, or seminar coming out every few weeks.

We have become so dependent on technology, that in our world of instantaneous feedback we forget that to be successful, one may need to reduce the texting and twittering and actually interact with people—armed with a firm foundation of management principles. These principles are grounded in communication, human dynamics, processes, and productivity.

When discussions come around as to how to be a success, the answers could fill a library. But most people are way too busy "doing it" to have time to read hundreds of books with theories on how to do it.

As a result, we published *The Inch Principle: 21 Million Dollar Inches of Management.* It's a compilation of successful principles of management that we have observed in the thousands of people our organization has trained and coached. These *Million Dollar Inches*, if applied in the workplace, can be major turning points to improved performance and maximum results.

When faced with tough challenges, instead of reaching in your top drawer for a pick-me-up or quick fix, try a *Million Dollar Inch*. When you do, you will feel comfort and inspiration. You will be energized, focused, and motivated to take action.

These principles go right to the heart of succeeding. They can be used in the order presented as an effective training blueprint for your operation, or they can be used on an as-needed basis to help in challenging situations.

John T. Condry
Paul E. Carpenter

MILLION DOLLAR INCH

Lesson at 30,000 Feet

A discovery is said to be an accident meeting a prepared mind.

- Albert Szent-Gyorgyiabout

On one of my many flights, I met a CEO from New York City. After we had exhausted the topics strangers usually discuss—the Yankees, Wall Street, the current administration—the discussion turned to business. This CEO was disgusted with the business climate of the day…in particular, lack of personal responsibility, excuses, backbiting, and inability to hit goals.

I probed a little deeper to see what he felt the solution to the problem was. It was something along the lines of, "The beatings will continue until morale improves around here."

Doubling his expectations to make up for the shortfall was not working for this executive. Human resources pointed the finger at management, so the CEO invested in an expensive four-day manager's retreat with a trendy training firm. The managers who attended gave the event a big thumbs-up and promised to change. But unfortunately, the concepts were too big and unrealistic to address their current challenges. The concepts fizzled out, and the retreat ended up being just another disappointing flavor of the month.

The CEO then asked me for some advice.

"For starters, stop trying to change your managers," I suggested. "In our experience **you can't change people, so try changing the way they do things.**"

I knew I had captured the CEO's interest when he began scribbling down my words on a cocktail napkin.

"Your retreat failed because you expected that it would change your managers *for* you," I continued. "The hard truth is, you can **never outsource your own success.** Change that comes from the outside rarely lasts."

By this time, I had the CEO's full attention. Now he was enthusiastically coming up with insights and actions based on the concepts I had just shared with him.

His enthusiasm was contagious. I almost hated to tell him that these headlines were no "Sham-wow" cure. They were just our peculiar way of creating a common language and short-coding what works.

"If my managers would act on these two headlines, it would be worth a million dollars to the company!" he exclaimed. "Where can I buy your book? I want one for everyone on my management team."

Book? Who has time to write a book?

Turns out, we do. The pilot's voice cut our conversation short, but as we were putting our seats into the upright and locked position, the *Million Dollar Inches* were already connecting together in my mind.

MILLION DOLLAR INCH

Introduction:
The Inch Principle

Ask any racer, any real racer. It doesn't matter if you win by an inch or a mile; winning's winning.

- The Fast and the Furious

The Inch Principle

I t is late in the fourth quarter of a high school championship football game. The score is tied ten to ten. The home team has the ball on their twenty-yard line. The first- and second-string quarterbacks are injured; the only one left is the third stringer, and he is terrible. Every time he throws the ball, it's an interception. Every time he hands off, he fumbles. But he *is* an excellent punter.

The coach grabs his third-string quarterback on the sideline and says, "We are going for the tie. We are going to run three quarterback sneaks and then punt. Do you understand? Three sneaks and punt!"

So the young man gets on the field, takes the first snap, and a huge hole opens up on the left side—he stumbles forward for a thirty-yard gain. Now the crowd is going crazy. There are forty seconds left. He takes the second snap, and another hole opens up. He stumbles down to the opponent's twenty-yard line. There are now about ten seconds left. The stadium is rocking with excitement. He takes his third snap and follows the center down to the one-inch line!

With one second left on the clock, the quarterback takes the snap and punts the ball out of the stadium. The fans and the players are in complete shock! The coach runs out onto the field, screaming at the kid, "What in the world were you thinking when you kicked the ball?" And the kid replied, "I was thinking what a stupid coach we have."

> ### *A slight edge of energy and concentration might be the difference between winning and losing.*

"Missed it by *that* much...." Agent Maxwell Smart held up his thumb and forefinger with an inch of space between them. Once again, he was describing a hopelessly misguided attempt to pull off a spectacular super-spy move. As management consultants, we constantly hear about make-or-break decisions where the margin is "*that* much."

Here Are a Few Examples

- An important hiring decision

- A decision to take the business in a certain direction

- Making a tough call to lay someone off

- A heart-to-heart conversation that changed a relationship

- Writing a business plan

- An e-mail tirade that could not be erased

- Listening to an employee's suggestion

- Responding to a client's request

- A restructure of the organization

- Trusting a person with the success of a project

- Attending a seminar that changed an entire team's outlook

- An inappropriate or ill-timed action that turned the team against management

- A misunderstanding of expectations and entitlements

- A choice to go in a direction management knew was wrong

To be an effective manager, you must pay attention to the details of verbal and non-verbal communication, human relations, culture, legal landscape, gut instinct, leadership, and learning within your organization. We are often told in management training that we are not to "sweat the small stuff"—that we are, instead, to take care of the big picture, and the small stuff will take care of itself. This, of course, in relationship to the day-to-day realization of our objectives, could not be further from the truth.

As you observe your work as a manager and leader, open your eyes to a fresh point of view. See clearly the incidents that have preceded positive and negative results. We think you'll be amazed to find that all controllable successes or failures have their roots in small, defining moments.

The Inch Principle in Action

At the end of Super Bowl XLIII, Ben Roethlisberger, quarterback for the Pittsburg Steelers, lofted a pass over three Arizona Cardinal defenders and into the back right corner of the end zone. Santonio Holmes stretched every inch of his five-foot-eleven frame to catch the ball. It was close—an inch either way could have been the difference. Officials went to an instant-replay review, and confirmed what every Steelers fan packed into Raymond James Stadium already knew—touchdown.

The winner's share was $73,000 per player and the loser's share was $38,000. The difference was $35,000 per player. With forty-five players on the active roster, that one inch ended up being worth $1,575,000.

In the movie *Any Given Sunday*, Al Pacino, as Coach Tony D'Amato, gives a wonderfully inspirational speech. The coach understands that a team is not a homogenous entity. It is a collection of individual successes, measured in inches, which are fundamentally connected.

> "On this team," he tells the team, "we tear ourselves and everyone else around us to pieces for that inch. We claw with our fingernails for that inch, because we know when we add up all those inches that they are going to make the difference between winning and losing! Between living and dying!"

MILLION DOLLAR INCH

TAKENOTE™
DRIVE YOUR SUCCESS WITH PROVEN RESULTS

The Inch Principle

Being an effective manager is truly a game of winning by inches. Attention to detail allows for slight adjustments, decisions, and actions made on a daily basis, which can have a major impact on the bottom line.

Managers are constantly complaining of seemingly minor and innocuous events that are quickly forgotten, only to surface later as lawsuits, confrontations, misunderstandings, failure, and major "drama." It seems that the smallest of actions in an organization can have prodigious ramifications.

Unquestionably, the lesson of the Million Dollar Inches tells us, if you want to achieve anything big, challenging, magnificent, or unprecedented in your management role, you and your team have to raise awareness of the Million Dollar Inches that confront you every day. Once you recognize the opportunities, you are required to make sound judgments. Although nothing is guaranteed, our experience tells us that effective decisions tip the scale in favor of positive outcomes. Success in business truly comes down to a few moments. Be ready to make yours count.

MILLION DOLLAR INCH

 # 1

Never Let Your Style Get In the Way of Your Success

Seventy-two percent of employees are open to a new career opportunity, and you might be the reason. More than four out of ten employees blame their bosses' management styles as the reason they would be willing to leave.

- Yahoo! Hot Jobs Annual Job Satisfaction Survey

A kindly supervisor sits at her desk with her head in her hands. How will she tell her under-performing employee to clear out his desk?

An angry, controlling manager wins a battle of wills with his top performer. But the employee leaves and is now his main competition.

A detailed, vigilant bookkeeper revises the company's most profitable client's buying plan for the sake of efficiency. It causes a major firestorm, and the customer threatens to leave.

The board decides that their charismatic CEO is a liability because he forgets meetings, refuses to rein in spending, and has told them point blank his opinion of their recommendations.

The Director, the Promoter, the Supervisor, the Sheriff—if you're a manager, one of these words probably describes you. It's your style, your predisposition, the main reason you succeed.

And it's also the main reason you don't.

Good decisions tend to come when you're enjoying yourself. You're in the zone, full of energy, and you draw from your own deep well to make the game slow down. This is you in your element—your natural management gift. And it motivates you to succeed, undiminished by outside influences.

But your natural management gift can get in the way of your success when it's applied improperly. A manager who is unwilling or unable to adjust his approach to people, processes, or problems as needed finds he is prone to poor decision making, and loses credibility and respect along the way.

Recognizing your natural management gifts is critical to your success— and each of us has primary and secondary gifts that make up our individual style.

Natural Management Gifts Overview

The Director

Some managers make decisions as easily as they breathe. When they speak, the thinking has already been done. There are no other votes, no other opinions. Since they manage from the top down, the only thing that really matters is the bottom line.

These are the Directors– they desire power and control.

Directors provide the energy, the drive, and the focus. They can separate business matters from personal feelings. A Director being single-minded, wins business and extracts viable solutions to unsolvable problems. A Director's take-no-prisoners attitude is essential to your company's growth and prosperity.

But there's a cost.

A Director's style is typically brutal and his path to achievement is littered with discarded ideas, bruised egos, and smoldering resentments. He constantly lands himself in hot water with human resources, runs afoul of countless government regulations, industry standards, supplier and customer agreements, and has a pathological need to touch everyone else's work. He doesn't see this as a problem. However, his stranglehold on the business deprives the company of the contributions of talented employees and ultimately threatens the success of the Director himself.

The Promoter

Some people are born to charm. They have a story for every occasion, an uncanny knack for saying the right thing at the right time, and a winning way with people. They are quick on their feet, creative in the face of difficulty, and bursting with ideas. They make difficult things look easy, whether it's motivating people, speaking off-the-cuff to a large crowd, or launching impossible projects with a flying start. And they do it all with an energy that prompts others to see them as truly gifted.

These are the Promoters– they are larger than life.

THE INCH PRINCIPLE ■ 21 MILLION DOLLAR INCHES OF MANAGEMENT

But crouching behind the legend is the liability. A Promoting manager's footloose style and constant genius attacks provide cover for avoiding the dreary work of follow-through. This leaves the Promoter relying on his natural ability rather than preparation, and using charm to deflect criticism.

Sooner or later, the Promoter will get caught faking it, and his credibility will be blown. His brilliance is dismissed as cleverness, his empathy as manipulative. Finance is the last field you'll find him in, because he always buys more than he needs, overpays for everything, and grants ludicrous terms. And at home, he often faces overwhelming debt and an incomprehensible lack of savings.

The Supervisor

Some managers believe that the whole really is greater than the sum of its parts. They value peace above conflict and prefer consistency to creativity. Their challenge of others' performance is cloaked in a non-threatening suggestion, and their highest goal is for things to run smoothly.

These are the Supervisors—conscience of the organization and Zen master to its employees.

Sounds ideal! Who wouldn't want a manager who listens to all sides, allows co-workers to save face, and is sensitive and fair to employees, customers, and suppliers? Supervisors are the champions of excellence and will always find ways to make the company effective and keep its leaders in line.

But Supervisors all too often become victims of their own principled approach. They trade leadership for friendship, draw only vague lines in the sand, and allow themselves to be pushed around. They sugarcoat situations that need to be addressed in a bid to avoid conflict.

The Supervisor is also naturally inclined to take a back seat, observing the team's performance instead of directing it from the driver's seat. He's overlooked because he works behind the scenes and beneath the radar.

All the Supervisor really wants is recognition without limelight. And when he doesn't get it, he goes postal over something no one else can even remember.

The Sheriff

Do you know a manager who takes pride in denying requests, catching violators, and generally ruining everyone's day? This manager is calm, detached, and unemotional. It's his job to prevent everyone else from destroying the company, and he uses evidence, numbers, principles, and logical assumptions to do it.

These are the Sheriffs – they want things done right.

Companies need Sheriff managers. They treat spreadsheets like gospel truth, can analyze profit and loss statements at a glance, and see problems that others can't. They live primarily inside their own minds, analyzing problems, identifying patterns, and composing logical explanations. If you ever want to know "why," ask a Sheriff.

> ### There are no good or bad management styles—only different situations.

But a Sheriff will wind up shooting himself in the foot—because life constructed from a spreadsheet bears little relevance to front-line issues of business. The major need to be "right" in every minor detail renders the Sheriff ineffectual in crisis management situations. And his lack of a personal touch will bring an organization grinding to a halt if a Sheriff is given more authority than he can handle.

A Sheriff's impersonal, "manage-by-memo" approach is usually the quickest way to crush morale and cause the company to lose valuable people and customers for the wrong reasons.

THE INCH PRINCIPLE ■ 21 MILLION DOLLAR INCHES OF MANAGEMENT

Natural Gifts Define Your Management Style

Unless you are brand new to the business world, chances are you have encountered someone in a management position who has allowed their style to get in the way of their success.

Six Ways Never to Let Your Style Get in the Way

1. Examine Your Own Natural Gifts of Management

Knowing what you don't know is the best place to start. Think back to experiences you have had. Take inventory of your successes and failures. You will probably find that you can now recognize how your natural gifts caused you to succeed, and times when they became a roadblock to success.

2. Surround Yourself with People Who Have Different Natural Styles

People with similar styles tend to gravitate together. They become cliquish and cut themselves off from different viewpoints and approaches. This causes unnecessary failure, stress, and miscommunication. Every natural gift has "blind spots." Surround yourself with people who have natural gifts in areas of management that you do not.

3. Read Books on How the Other Half Lives

Directors should read *The 7 Habits of Highly Effective People* or *Who Moved My Cheese*. Promoters should read anything on how to manage your money and stay organized; Supervisor's should read *The Art of War* or a biography of any great leader. Sheriff's should read anything about marketing and *How to Win Friends and Influence People*.

4. Refrain from "Nicknames"

People at work tend to label others based on their natural gifts profile. Most of this goes on behind the persons back. Nicknames are part and parcel of business life. One Director had the nickname of "WOW," which stood for "Witch on Wheels." In one company, an entire compliance department was labeled the "sales prevention department." Realize that people's emotions drive their behaviors and in turn determine results. So apply common sense.

5. Learn to Listen and Understand Others

The secret to being successful in any leadership position is to relate to, communicate with and honestly access people. Never judge people on their natural style, instead judge on the content and quality of the work product.

6. Put Your People First

The bottom line about being an effective leader is this: "If you build your people, they will build your business." Every successful leader must learn how to train, support and motivate his or her team. If you don't take the time to support people and address their needs, your work will be useless.

Never Let Your Style Get In the Way of Your Success

Your natural management gifts define your management style—whether you realize it or not. But when you recognize what makes you sing and what sucks the life out of you, you're better equipped to handle people and situations that run counter to your most instinctive style.

That alone will make you a more effective leader. But when you can deploy your people in a way that makes the most of their gifts, you'll reap the benefits, as one person's life-draining chores becomes another's energizing challenge.

MILLION
DOLLAR INCH
 # 2

Steal a Play from Someone Else's Playbook

If you want to be successful, find someone who has achieved the results you want and copy what they do and you'll achieve the same results.

- Anthony Robbins

A rookie is set to return the opening kick-off in his first NFL exhibition game. He catches the ball in the end zone, runs it out to the two-yard line, and finds himself right in the path of a huge lineman barreling down on him. The rookie, realizing his mistake, steps back into the end zone and scores a touchback—two points...for the other team!

The rookie hangs his head, a miserable failure, and heads back to the bench. He knows he is due to be chewed out by the coach. But the coach realizes that a demanding response is not what's called for, and surprises the rookie by saying to him, "Cheer up son, it's not everybody who scores the first time they touch the ball!"

If only every manager could recognize situations in which his or her approach is ineffective and someone else's is better!

As an executive, you are paid for your ability to perform in a variety of roles. But that doesn't mean you give them equal time or attention. Naturally, it's more rewarding to manage mostly in areas that play to your strengths, and to avoid or ignore those areas that expose your weakness. But sooner or later, an effective leader is going to have to find a way to bring things into balance.

This is where stealing a page from someone else's playbook could become a regular management tool.

He's Just Not That Into You

Early in my career, I had the inside track on a promotion. I was excited about where I was going when the owner of the company called me into his office. Anticipating advancement, I was stunned when he told me that I was not the man for the job.

"I need someone who is willing to make unpopular decisions and hold people accountable," the boss explained. "In this position, the higher up you go, the less popular you're going to be—and that's just not you."

I was shocked, angry, and frustrated. I wanted to quit. I had been passed over not because of my performance, but because of my style.

Yet eventually, I found myself agreeing with him, and I resigned myself to the role of coach, consultant, teacher, motivator, and relationship builder. I would have to leave the tough accountability job to someone else.

I Came, I Saw, I Learned

Years later, I was doing consulting work for a company. When the owner started the company a few years prior, he had vigorously recruited a young man whom he was grooming as his successor. Six years into the relationship, the young man announced that he was going to take another opportunity with a current client.

The owner reminded the young man that he had signed an agreement forbidding such an action. "I understand your wish to work elsewhere," the boss told him, "but the discussion is closed. Your only option is to buy your agreement out." Even under intense pressure from the client, other employees, his wife, and of course, his apprentice, the owner stood his ground. And although he had to beg, borrow, and steal to buy out his agreement, the young man finally did.

This event was fresh in my mind when a client called me to cancel our training agreement. "I need to remind you that we have an agreement," I told my client. "I understand your issue, but the discussion is closed."

> ## *The more you know about how other people operate, the easier it is to adapt.*

I couldn't believe I was saying those words! He was stunned, and so was I.

For the next twenty-four hours, I wanted to pick up the phone and say, "Look, it's OK, buddy. No worries about the agreement." But instead, I "stole" a page out of my other client's playbook. After a tense day of waiting, I finally heard back. My client was going to honor our agreement.

I'm Not Superman

When you're faced with a "kryptonite" situation, we suggest you "temporarily" steal a page out of the playbook of someone who breezes right through similar circumstances. Using the four natural management gifts as a guide, you can get a feel for the kind of things such people do well. Talk to them, find out exactly how they do it...and then adjust your approach.

This doesn't mean outsourcing your success. You are not trying to be someone you are not. You won't fool anyone, anyway. But the more you know about utilizing other natural gifts, the easier it will be for you to adapt those behaviors into a situation where you may be out of your natural element.

Steal a Page from a Prime Example

The Director

If it's your nature to avoid dealing openly with consequential situations, steal a page from the Director's playbook. Directors are confident in their decision making, comfortable with the outcomes, and able to meet do-or-die challenges head-on without wavering. You might not be able to act like a Director, but you can work at putting things out in the open with your team in a controlled setting where problems, priorities, and results are addressed and resolved in one sitting.

The Promoter

If you have a hard time relating to the whole idea of external motivation, the Promoter's playbook has some ideas you can use. Promoters are naturals at publicly recognizing good performance and are adept at the sort of internal marketing that inspires and motivates people. So learn to look for incremental success, and call it out. Everyone already knows you're not a Promoter, so even a small positive stroke from someone like you can have a big impact.

The Supervisor

The Supervisor's playbook has words of wisdom for those of you who find monitoring day-to-day, item-oriented progress too tedious for words. Supervisors have a natural gift for "hand holding," and they are excellent mediators who frequently check on others' personal and profession progress. You'll never develop the Supervisor's patience for managing inexperienced employees, but you can set the boundaries that they come by naturally. No good news, no bad news, no drama—just information and fewer surprises.

The Sheriff

If you're a big-picture person with little use for the gory details, steal a page from the Sheriff's playbook book. Sheriffs play by the rules. They live on facts and finance and are driven by logic and consistency, and they actively seek to "out" non-compliance. No one will ever mistake you for a Sheriff, but his handy tool—a spreadsheet—can be used occasionally to threaten your team into sending up useful summaries.

> ## *Get gifted people on your speed dial.*

Managing our own weak areas is exhausting work. But this Million Dollar Inch gives you a way to sidestep the conflict of fighting your own nature by helping you incorporate the successful styles of others into your own routine.

Get to know the natural gifts of everyone in your inner circle. Check your ego at the door, and learn to access people when you are out of your element. Organize them on your speed dial according to gifts, and don't be afraid to call in a lifeline.

THE INCH PRINCIPLE ■ 21 MILLION DOLLAR INCHES OF MANAGEMENT

Steal a Page from Someone Else's Playbook

People don't generally burn out by doing work they enjoy—they burn out because they're not doing enough of it.

To be successful in the long run, your company needs leaders who can survive the trip. Rather than bulldozing your way through "kryptonite" situations, spend some time building up your weaker natural management gifts—and steal some plays from others.

More time and effort isn't the answer. Learning a few unfamiliar techniques and incorporating them into your own approach is a continuous learning process. The process allows you to borrow successful behavior from the gifted, but stop short of outsourcing your own success.

MILLION DOLLAR INCH

3

Don't Change You—Change the Way You Do Things

■ *CEO: So, it sounds like you have dealt with things like this in your career before.*

Consultant: Yes, many times.

CEO: So what was your solution?

Consultant: I quit the job to become a consultant!

E ver tried to get one of your company's long-timers to try something new? If he's convinced the old thing is better, it's nearly impossible.

That's because genuine change is hard to come by. People are stubborn; just look through any history book, and you'll find dozens who chose death over change. Memo to the senior vice president who invests his precious energy and resources to convince his organization that "*change is the ticket*"—good luck!

People don't change.

They may adjust their behavior in order to fit in, achieve pleasure or avoid pain. But if you're waiting for them to see the light, you might as well get comfortable. Better yet, just retire from the changing business altogether— you're out of your league.

Don't bother asking why. It's a human condition. And left untreated, it morphs into a subtle resistance that spreads through your organization in the form of small "victories" over management. You'll have to lower your expectations and realize that from a practical standpoint, getting people to do things your way is almost as good as getting them to see things your way—and it's a lot easier.

> *Getting people to do things your way is almost as good as getting them to see things your way—and it's a lot easier.*

Under the circumstances, you might think management would be content with incremental changes in behavior. Oddly enough, many managers prefer to beat their heads against the wall with sweeping programs that seek to change an employee's soul—or at least his heart—in the cause of greater productivity and deeper job satisfaction.

It's important for managers to see how little there is to be gained by waging a war of wills against those who refuse to change. In fact, your own well-being and effectiveness may be at stake. It is better to focus on getting someone to try something new in spite of his negative opinions. At least you stand a chance of producing acceptable behavior.

You can start by understanding why people find it so difficult to change.

Here Are Four Things You Should Know and Apply

1. What we see in others and what they see in themselves are not the same. It is vital that we report our perceptions objectively and fairly.

2. We've all been hard-wired from early on. It took us time to perfect these habits, so changing them permanently will not be easy.

3. Sometimes people are aware of their ineffective behavior, but they still don't change when the reward for staying the same outweighs the risk of changing.

4. Management creates resistance by applying obvious manipulation techniques.

The key word for your recalcitrant employees is "try"—not "try harder," but "try this."

An effective adjustment can be anything that provides a way or a reason to change, while monitoring progress or lack of it.

Try These Tools

✔ Schedule	✔ Process
✔ Procedure	✔ New Technology
✔ Technique	✔ Reminder
✔ Checklist	✔ Cheat sheet
✔ Incentive	✔ Cross-training
✔ Mentor	✔ Repercussion
✔ Accountability	✔ Visual Tracking
✔ Block Out Time	

When you offer a way to adjust behavior, you put responsibility for the choice where it belongs—squarely in the other person's lap. You must make your intentions and reasoning clear. You must encourage people to come up with their own adjustments (or put their stamp on yours). You must mandate the behavior adjustment and clearly state the cost of deviation. And most importantly, you must follow through.

You can't save everyone, but how you handle the change issue makes a big impact for the rest. You'll earn more support from your employee base if you fire someone because of his inability to perform, rather than his failure to change his beliefs or personality.

The power to adjust is in your hands!

MILLION DOLLAR INCH

3

TAKENOTE™

DRIVE YOUR SUCCESS WITH PROVEN RESULTS

Don't Change You—Change the Way You Do Things

Any serious attempt to change the way things are done throughout an organization is not a project for the faint of heart. It will extract a toll in the form of money and human effort, because the people who need to change the most are the ones who change the least.

Introduce behavior adjustments that lead to performance improvements to avoid losing the right people for the wrong reasons. Communicate your expectations in an objective, non-emotional way; leave your anger, cheerleading, simmering, and lecturing at the door, and coach your people in ways that allow them to change their own minds.

When you do, change takes hold and spreads among your good people. And increased productivity will arrive sooner and at a much lower cost.

MILLION DOLLAR INCH

4

1   2   3   4   5

Stop Looking for Solutions—
Start Treating the Condition

Assistant: Our CEO would like to look a little thinner
for the cover of this year's annual report.
How far can you back up?

Photographer: How's Alaska?

P ersonality conflicts, morale issues, communication breakdowns, financial concerns, hiring and firing, and personal drama...no matter what we do, some problems never seem to go away.

And maybe they weren't meant to.

In 2009, President George W. Bush left office in the midst of a global financial crisis. Before he left, he tried to soothe America's troubled minds by explaining that "...anxiety can feed anxiety, and that can make it hard to see all that's being done to solve the problem."

But somehow that exhortation didn't do much to calm our fears over our financial futures. And it's because people know that their anxiety over the economic crisis is not a problem that's easily solved. In fact, it's not a problem at all—it's a *condition*.

Conditions are, by their nature, a collection of many moving parts that need to be addressed. Problems can be solved with one universal answer—a "miracle cure"—that will offer a solution to keep the problem from ever darkening our doors again. But when you treat a *condition*, you accept the reality that you will be dealing with it forever.

> *Problems come and go. But when you treat a condition, you accept the reality that you will be dealing with it forever.*

Try to get over the shock!

It's time to face the reality; most everyday management challenges have no solution. No universal answers will cure your management problems for good. And even if there were such a thing, you wouldn't have time to find them.

I Want Some Answers

Ten years ago, my daughter was diagnosed with Hodgkin's disease. I was on the road and returned immediately to meet my family at the oncologist's office, my head full of questions…*How will she feel in a week? Six months? A year? What will happen next? Are there any guarantees?* **And how could this have happened?**

My wife, however, had moved ahead. She was already discussing treatments, counseling, schoolwork, and finances. At one point in the meeting, she finally had to tell me, "We need you to stop asking questions and help manage our daughter's condition. There are no answers. There is just treatment. If you're not with us, I can't use you."

My daughter has been in remission for many years, but the lesson I learned that day still stays with me: success in management must begin with a fundamental change in my own attitude. There is no magic bullet. There is no corporate Camelot. Eventually, we must stop looking for answers and start understanding the long-term nature of the challenge.

That's not an easy pill to swallow for problem-solvers and dreamers.

> *There are no universal answers that will cure your management problems for good.*

But when you begin to see that problems aren't really isolated cases of bad luck, lousy timing, or dumb ideas, you begin to take on the long view. You re-classify problems as conditions—perennial conditions—that increase your awareness and ability to help your team make it better. And that is the beginning of success.

It won't be easy, of course. The fat cats who are profiting regardless of the expense to the business will not be happy. Your new treatment plan will take everyone out of their comfort zones, and force them to give up their complacency or get out of the way. Managers who see themselves as primarily problem solvers will be vexed in their pursuit of corporate Utopia. But nothing—and no one— is untouchable.

How to Treat a Condition

• Commit for the long haul

• Gather data and determine possible treatment plans

• Recruit as many people as you can for the "treatment team"

• Determine the critical areas to start applying effective management

• Evaluate your support and resources

• Implement the treatment plan

• Monitor status and track results

• Be open to adjusting the plan as necessary

Even though my daughter is in remission, her doctors no longer need to micro-manage her condition, but she still goes in for periodic exams. These check-ups are a precautionary measure, but they help her doctors make adjustments if they discover any changes.

You'll have to monitor your team, too. Applying this principle will help you remember that workplace life is an interesting, imperfect, long-term condition, always in some stage of symptom or remission. And over time, you will become wise to the conditions and adept at the treatment.

MILLION DOLLAR INCH #4

TAKENOTE™
DRIVE YOUR SUCCESS WITH PROVEN RESULTS

Stop Looking for Solutions—Start Treating the Condition

Recognizing that problems are really conditions will unlock a whole new perspective for executives. Rather than allowing expensive "solutions" to undermine future results, effective leaders will evaluate a condition for what it really is and focus on an attainable treatment for it.

Once a condition is known, acknowledged, and treated, day-to-day challenges will no longer drain managers of their vision, enthusiasm, and commitment to goals. And re-positioning goals as treatments for ongoing conditions will lead to monitoring, maintenance, and eventually, improvement.

THE INCH PRINCIPLE ■ 21 MILLION DOLLAR INCHES OF MANAGEMENT

MILLION DOLLAR INCH

5

If It's Not an Exact Science, Play the Percentages

Poker must be viewed as one long lifetime game instead of many short sessions. The reason for this is over the course of thousands of hands, the best hand will win the correct amount of time. Poker, however, is full of short-term variance (often called luck), which can be extremely frustrating. Despite losing when the odds are overwhelmingly in your favor, the goal of winning poker is still to put yourself in this type of situation as many times as possible because when you do, you will win most of the time.

- Wesley R. Young
  "How to Calculate Poker Odds"

A wealthy Texas businessman with a less-than-desirable daughter invited the town's eligible young bachelors to his ranch. The fifteen-hundred-acre spread afforded every luxury a billionaire could wish for.

The businessman gathered his young guests around his giant swimming pool filled with alligators. He explained the purpose for their visit, "I value courage more than anything," he said. "It is what made me a billionaire. The man with enough courage to jump in that pool and swim to the other side will receive half my land, half my money, or the hand of my beautiful daughter, who will one day inherit it all."

Moments later, a splash was heard as one of the bachelors swam for his life, staying just inches ahead of the hungry gators. The crowd was amazed as he pulled himself unharmed from the pool.

The billionaire was astonished, but stuck to his promise. "You are a man of courage, and you may have anything you want," he said. "The land, the money, my daughter..."

The exhausted swimmer shook his head. "All I want," he said, "is to know the name of the guy who pushed me into the pool."

In business, some things are fairly certain. But precise measurements and precise outcomes that can be reproduced over and over without fail rarely happen. Instead—surprise!—you probably find yourself pushed into a pool of alligators on a regular basis.

That's why a successful leader gets comfortable playing the percentages; he simply takes the better chance. While some things are reliable (a departmental budget shortfall will always raise questions, for example), dozens of variables make most management situations far less predictable. A good manager will remember that he is dealing with people, timing, internal and external competition, and a host of other unknowns.

Playing the percentages is also known as the "smart play," and for good reason. While there are no foolproof formulas for making the right management decision every time, in the long run, "smart players" will be right more often than they're wrong.

So why don't more managers play the percentages?

Some see themselves as risk-takers and prefer to place their bets on a bigger win. Others don't trust the odds, passing up almost-right opportunities in the hopes that the perfect moment is just around the corner. But most often, managers simply don't have the information they need to choose the smart play.

> ### *Going against the percentages is a sure sign that you're short of useful information.*

With all of the data available these days, it hardly seems possible to blame poor choices on a lack of information. But that's exactly what happens. Sometimes there is too much information to be useful, and it's easier (and possibly safer) to just ignore it all. Information becomes homogenous—the same raw data is just cranked through different modes. And of course, management "tools" are attractively packaged as exact science, when nothing could be further from the truth.

Works 100 Percent of the Time, Guaranteed

A hiring manager I know called me to complain about an expensive evaluation she had been using. Its purpose was to screen candidates for senior sales positions. "This thing isn't working!" she said. "It's guaranteed to tell me whether someone can sell or not. A couple of people it green-lighted turned out to be thieves, and it didn't even recommend two of the best people I hired. What good is this thing?"

I'm familiar with this particular tool, and it can yield remarkable insights. But it's not guaranteed. That was a risk my friend took. The percentage play would be to back up the evaluation with common sense hiring practices, such as second interviews, reference checks, case studies, and contact in personal settings. That's exactly how my friend ended up with her two star hires. Statistics tell us that one interview and a profile will yield the right choice about 16 percent of the time—not exactly a betting hand.

It turns out that hiring the right person is far from an exact science, and the best evaluation tool in the world can't change that.

The gut instinct school would have us believe that judgment is guesswork informed by experience and intuition. And when managers make gut choices that are successful, they are often viewed as prodigies—as unconventional stars.

> *Once you remove ego and emotion,*
> *the percentage play is usually clear.*

Playing the percentages forces you to do your homework—to gather useful information, to back it up with the tried and true, and to find things out for yourself. There will still be times when you take a wrong turn. But when you make choices based on the best odds, you'll know you gave yourself the best chance to succeed.

If It's Not an Exact Science, Play the Percentages

Playing the percentages in business is less about outrunning the bear, and more about outrunning the camper next to you.

The "experience" from which smart decisions are thought to flow is really nothing more than the accumulated lessons from the decisions that have gone before. A savvy manager will keep track of the results of her choices—good and bad—in order to improve the chances that her next decision will be the right one.

Over time, the ability to be consistently closer to the mark than either your rivals or your competitors translates into a tremendous advantage for your company. And ultimately, better decisions always lead to better results.

MILLION DOLLAR INCH

6

1 2 3 4 5

Never Outsource Your Own Success

Bill: Wyld Stallyns will never be a super band until we have Eddie Van Halen on guitar.

Ted: I do not believe we will get Eddie Van Halen until we have a triumphant video.

Bill: Ted, it's pointless to have a triumphant video before we have decent instruments.

Ted: How can we have decent instruments when we don't know how to play?

Bill: That is why we NEED Eddie Van Halen!

Ted: And THAT is why we need a triumphant video.

Bill, Ted: EXCELLENT!

- Bill & Ted's Excellent Adventure

Decisiveness is an essential aspect of leadership. No one will follow someone who freezes in the midst of a crisis. No one appreciates a leader who cannot make decisions without the approval of others. And no one respects a leader who makes a decision, and then constantly second-guesses that decision. People respect a decisive leader.

Maybe that pressure is what drives managers to turn to the enormous market for shortcuts to success in business management today. Managers tend to be easy targets for that extra tip or technique that promises to turn all their potential into bottom-line results.

However, relying on outside resources when making important decisions about what to do or not to do in your particular situation usually ends in failure.

Remember *Happy Days*, the iconic TV sitcom set in the 1950's? When mild-mannered Richie Cunningham is confronted by bullies at the diner, he turns to the Fonz for help. But even after Richie masters the moves, the swagger, and the attitude—even the leather jacket—his attempts to ward off the bullies still fall short. It seems the Fonz had forgotten one important element in Richie's education: sometimes, you actually have to hit someone.

> *Some people will die before changing a belief, but ideas should always be subject to updating, adapting, and adjusting.*

It's one thing to get training, help, or advice. But managers who believe they can outsource the central components of their success will end up revealing their lack of self-confidence and real-world application. And when self-confidence is lacking, none of the bailouts, fads, parables, management gurus, research, and business superstars will make a difference.

So what's your Fonz? What beliefs are central to your decision making? What formulas have lulled you into thinking they are fool-proof every time? Until you cancel your membership in someone else's belief club, your ability to think for yourself is cut off.

For many managers, their Fonz takes the form of a belief that is central to their decision making. I agree with Chris Rock, the comedian, who in commenting on beliefs in his stand-up act says that people should exchange beliefs for ideas. Rock says people will die before changing a belief, but ideas can be updated, adapted, and adjusted based on circumstances. When we join the "cult" of someone's belief, we, in essence, cut off our ability to think for ourselves. Even in the face of a current reality, management will allow false beliefs to stop them from seeing situations for what they truly are. The goal in a leadership position is to make decisions based on current reality, sound principals, and ideas. We want to move away from decision making based on a formula that we were taught by our Fonz to believe is workable in every situation.

Managers who try to outsource their success many times feel an allegiance to their Fonz, and cling to a false belief in an effort to show their support. At some point, managers must break with the chains that bind them to failure and think for themselves. In the comedy *Talladega Nights: The Legend of Ricky Bobby*, NASCAR star Ricky has based his life on a single comment his charismatic dad made at career day when he was twelve. Reese Bobby said, "If you are not first, you're last." Later in life, this belief was no longer working for Ricky. Down on his luck, he confronted his Father:

Ricky Bobby: "Wait, Dad. Don't you remember the time you told me "If you ain't first, you're last"?

Reese Bobby: Huh? What are you talking about, Son?

Ricky Bobby: That day at school.

Reese Bobby: Oh heck, Son, I was high that day. That doesn't make any sense at all, you can be second, third, and fourth...you can even be fifth.

<u>Ricky Bobby</u>: What? I've lived my whole life by that!

Six Ideas on Decision Making

1. Assumption is the Mother of All Mistakes

Before you can start to make decisions, you need to be absolutely clear on the issue. Write it down in a sentence and clear the debris of influence from others surrounding it.

2. Assess the Consequences

All decisions have implications for you, the team and your company. When you consider others, choose building an alliance over consent. Consent involves total agreement with everyone before moving forward. Instead, build alliances where you discuss decisions, but the leader makes the final decision. People don't necessarily have to agree with the leader, but they must at least agree to support the decision so things can move forward.

3. Explore Different Viewpoints

Viewpoints are simply different lenses through which you look at the issues at hand. By exploring different viewpoints, you start to get a feel for those that make sense for your situation.

4. Best Case – Worst Case

When you are faced with a big decision, it is easy to get lost in the detail and circumstances. An alternative is to get clear on your ideal outcome and use this ideal outcome to inform your choices.

5. Ben Franklin Exercise

Another way of looking at a decision is to consider the advantages and disadvantages of each of the options open to you. Simply listing the advantages and disadvantages of each option is a powerful way of moving forward on decisions.

The Ben Franklin Exercise:

1. *Make two columns by drawing a vertical line in the middle of a page.*

2. *Under column one, brainstorm and write down all the advantages.*

3. *Under column two, brainstorm and write down all the disadvantages.*

4. *Start making trade-offs—if items under each side have equal value, then cross them out.*

5. *Continue this exercise until one column is completely crossed out; this means the remaining column has the advantage.*

6. Learn from Everyone, Decide for You

Frank Perdue was a Maryland farmer who revolutionized the American poultry industry with the introduction of his brand-name chickens, transforming a backyard egg business into one of the nation's largest food companies.

The first hands-on CEO to become famous as a company advertising spokesperson, he appeared in approximately two hundred television commercials. Frank Perdue's stubborn commitment to learn from all the experts on Madison Avenue led to the creation of one of modern advertising's most memorable lines, "It takes a tough man to make a tender chicken."

Frank Perdue cold called agency after agency and was relentless in his pursuit of information from any expert willing to share. Then, he made his own decision. Frank attributed his success to determination, hard work, honest dealings, innovative marketing and, perhaps most importantly, an obsession with learning from everyone.

THE INCH PRINCIPLE ■ 21 MILLION DOLLAR INCHES OF MANAGEMENT

Never Outsource Your Own Success

Looking beyond ourselves for success in business almost always brings disappointment.

A manager who understands why a principle works can then take responsibility for success or failure of the application. The manager who isn't responsible for his own ideas should be identified and replaced.

Designing one's own blueprint for success based on your company's unique needs means that the lack of self-confidence and real-world application will finally be eliminated. In its place will be an energizing and contagious work environment that can only lead to success.

MILLION DOLLAR INCH

7

1 2 3 4 5

Nothing Happens without Personal Responsibility

Let everyone sweep in front of his own door, and the whole world will be clean.

- Johann Wolfgang Von Goethe

A woman sues a furniture store after she trips over a misbehaving toddler and breaks her ankle. The toddler in question? Her own son.

A burglar is locked in a garage he is trying to burgle. He sues the vacationing homeowners after being forced to live on dog food and warm Pepsi for the eight days he is trapped there.

A man's thirty-two-foot RV crashes when he sets it to cruise control and goes to make a sandwich—while the RV is moving. He sues the manufacturer, claiming that the owner's manual didn't specify that he needed to stay at the wheel.

Personal responsibility—we hear about it a lot. In business, it usually comes from the top down, and you will run into it most often in one of two ways.

First, an organization's management will communicate downward its desire for everyone else to take ownership for (fill in the blank). Unfortunately, the other time you hear about taking personal responsibility is when a political or corporate figure has failed to do it. You don't have to think too hard to come up with a disgraced politician or CEO who has said these very words while insisting he still deserves to keep his job.

What is Personal Responsibility?

For starters, it's not just an urban legend about a careless RV driver. As a manager, you probably see it every day—too many people believe that they should not be held responsible for the choices they make, nor should they accept the consequences of choices gone badly. Someone will always come along to let them off the hook.

> *Most people won't step up and take responsibility—why risk it?*

But the great thing about taking personal responsibility is that it's personal. There's no need to take a cue from those upper managers who don't do it themselves. Don't wait for a memo or policy paper. You can do it any time you like. And if, as a manager, you are willing to set the tone, one team dedicated to accepting personal responsibility for its work can turn an entire company around. That's making something happen!

So where do you start? First, realize that most people want to take responsibility, at least for their own work. Given a chance, they believe they'll succeed, and they hope for both a paycheck and credit for their success in return.

The biggest roadblock to your new "responsibility drive" is fear...and fear is mostly uncertainty. Will I lose my job? Will I be humiliated? Will I lose my title or office? What will other people think?

Resentment, apathy, and office politics follow—do you want to play mind games, or do you want to get things done? Take away the fear, and there's nothing but clear thinking ahead!

After you dispel the fear, it's time to address ownership—a concept that has been largely misapplied by the corporate world. It's a concept that forgets to include a very important part: take ownership, but also understand the consequences of decisions you make. To own something is to have the freedom to decide its fate. If your team members don't have this freedom, there's nothing for which they can claim responsibility.

> ## *To own something is to have the freedom to decide its fate.*

Taking personal responsibility also gives your team permission to challenge the status quo and to diminish the false pride that is the downfall of so many companies. Since a manager's number one goal is to achieve results, no one on the team can be afraid to challenge a decision.

THE INCH PRINCIPLE ■ 21 MILLION DOLLAR INCHES OF MANAGEMENT

When people have the freedom, they feel the ownership, and with that ownership, a sense of responsibility and a far better grasp of the consequences of failure and success. Of course, you do an employee no favors by allowing him or her to continue failing without some intervention. But ask any entrepreneur: failing on one's own is often a prelude to success.

And don't forget to reward that success!

Nothing Happens without Personal Responsibility

Apply this Million Dollar Inch, and get ready to see the direct relationship between personal responsibility and success! Your team's most valuable players are the ones who accept responsibility, who challenge the status quo, who shy away from game playing, and who seldom play it safe. You want as many of these "fools" or "heroes" on your team as you can get!

When you begin to trade freedom of ownership for responsibility among your team, you'll find yourself with a bumper crop of heroes, and everyone will enjoy the fruits of their considerable labor.

MILLION
DOLLAR INCH
8

Create a Balance of Power with Today's Workforce

I suppose leadership at one time meant muscles, but today it means getting along with people.

- Gandhi

An important Army officer called the motor pool to secure transportation for the weekend. An enthusiastic young man ran through the list of options.

"We've got Jeeps for the sergeants and lieutenants, command cars for captains and colonels, and for Old Fatty, the general, we have a big black Cadillac.

"Do you know who this is speaking, young man?" said the officer.

"Nope," said the dispatcher.

"This is the general."

After a long pause, the dispatcher spoke. "Do you know who this is?"

The general said, "No."

"Then so long, Fatty!"

Power is the ability to insist upon or resist a situation. If you can hire, fire, reward, control access or information, create a need to succeed, or in any other way control someone's economic well-being or freedom, you can exercise "external" power over him.

But your employees have power, too. If they claim discrimination, retaliation, exercise entitlement, have talents you can't do without, or find out proprietary information, management's external power will be neutralized.

> ## *With great power comes great responsibility.*

And what ensues is a giant waste of time, money, energy, and effort—also known as a power-play between management expectations and employee entitlements.

Management Power-Play Book Revealed

Social psychologists French and Raven, in a now-classic study (1959) developed a schema of six categories of power that power-holders rely upon to compel acquiescence.

Authority...is the power of an individual relative to his position and duties within an organization. Legitimate power is a formal authority that has been assigned to a person within a particular position.

Charisma...is a person's power or ability to attract others and build loyalty. It's based on the interpersonal skills of the power holder. In this instance, someone who is influenced by charisma wants to identify with these qualities, and gains satisfaction from being an accepted follower.

Expertise...is the power when a person's skills match an organization's need for those skills. Unlike other types of power, expertise is usually highly specific and is limited to the particular area in which the expert is trained and qualified.

Information...is power held by those who are well versed, up-to-date, and able to persuade others. Those who hold the power of information have access to inside details. They do not have a strict need to look the part of the professional, but they must keep current with new research, technology, and advances in their profession.

Reward Power...depends on the ability of the power holder to confer valued material benefits. It is the degree to which the individual can give such incentives as time off, benefits, desired gifts, promotions, or increases in pay or responsibility. This power is obvious, but it is also ineffective if it is abused. Those who misuse reward power can become too pushy, or may be criticized for being too forthcoming or for moving things too quickly.

Coercion..is the application of negative influences upon employees. It might refer to the ability to demote or to withhold other rewards. Coercion is the desire for valued rewards or the fear of having them with-held to enforce the obedience of those under power. Coercive power is

THE INCH PRINCIPLE ▦ 21 MILLION DOLLAR INCHES OF MANAGEMENT

the most obvious—but least effective—form of power, because it builds resentment and resistance.

Employees Strike Back

Managers aren't the only ones who wield external power in a workplace setting. There are four workplace developments that give employees power too.

The Speed of Information...affects nearly all aspects of working life. The technological advances of the last few decades have revolutionized business, especially as people can reach others around the world in a matter of seconds, with minimal cost. As technology improves, managers find it increasingly difficult to control the flow or confidentiality of information in the workplace.

My daughter was once caught up in a dramatic episode at school. I left work to pick her up with my wife's mandate ringing in my ears: I was not to alert my daughter to my impending arrival, because she might leave campus in her current state of mind.

As I crossed the school parking lot, I passed one of my daughter's friends. Two steps later, my phone rang. It was my wife. "Mary knows you're on campus," she said. "How did that happen?"

It seems my daughter's friend alerted my daughter that I was on campus via text message. My daughter then texted my wife: "Why is Dad here?" Wow! When information can travel that quickly, it's hard to stay in control of any situation, especially one in which the element of surprise is your best management approach.

Anti-Discrimination...guidelines demand that managers be innocent of considering protected characteristics such as race, religion, gender, national origin, age, citizenship, pregnancy, or physical disability. In addition to these federal anti-discrimination rules, state laws may cover some businesses exempt from the federal laws or provide additional protections for such details as sexual orientation or marital status. As a manager, you are required to base all management decisions on relevant employment characteristics and job performance only.

A failure to not consider all of these protected details could land you in legal trouble. And the cost is great. Not only will lawyers' costs, fines or damages, court costs, and even the employee's legal fees add up, but lost productivity as your business is tied up in investigations will only bring bad publicity and will damage morale.

Entitlement...is the rallying cry of those who feel they deserve everything without actually having to work for it. Hopefully, your team is made up of those who bring a great deal of talent, energy, and technical savvy to the workplace. But probably a few of these talented folks are also impatient, self-serving, disloyal, and unable to delay gratification. In an "I deserve it!" workplace atmosphere, a manager can lose her ability to motivate and keep harmony on the team.

Job Hopping...in years past, employees were reluctant to fight the powers that be for fear of being labeled a "job hopper" if they left. This forced them to figure out how to work within the system. But today, it's commonplace to be employed by three or more companies in a career. Potential employers look at a résumé as a lifestyle, and are anxious to re-label the expertise that has been paid for by someone else as "ambition."

Create a Balance of Power

Instead of expensive and time-consuming power struggles, follow this alternative strategy of communication and action:

1. **Establish clear standards and objectives** – Each person should be able to answer the question, **"What does management expect me to accomplish?"**

2. **Incentive is the key to success** – Incentive is the force that propels high performance. Each person should be able to answer the question, **"What's in it for me?"**

3. **Consistent performance appraisals** – Effective appraisals are progress reports on accomplishing agreed-upon objectives. Each person should be able to answer the question, **"How am I doing, Coach?"**

4. **Benchmarks** – Benchmarks indicate what must happen for people to achieve their objective. Each person should be able to answer the question, **"What indicators tell me I have been or will be successful?"**

5. **Proficiency** – Proficiency is the knowledge, skill, and ability to achieve your objectives. Each person should be able to answer the question, **"How do I improve?"**

6. **Capital** – Capital is the tools, technology, training, and resources available to achieve objectives. Each person should be able to answer the question, **"What resources are available to me?"**

7. **Freedom** – Without the freedom to perform, power struggles are inevitable. Each person should be able to answer the question, **"What can I do in the time available to me that someone like me is allowed to do?"**

Create a Balance of Power with Today's Workforce

Your goal as a manager—and this can be difficult—is to achieve a balance of power between management and your workforce. This leads to a consistent work product.

Managers have five elements of power to utilize, but remember that employees have elements of power that can cause a struggle too. You'll keep those expensive and time-consuming power struggles in check if you encourage leadership on both sides (through education, common sense, personal responsibility, and precise communication) .

When you create a balance of power, stop abuses of that power, and create a management structure that allows employees to communicate concerns without a power struggle, your entire team will be effective.

MILLION DOLLAR INCH

9

Graduate from a Day Care to an Adult Learning Center

Attention, all idiotic morons! Yes, that means you!

- Memo from an angry executive to his team

Ever seen someone melt down before your eyes? A vice president of operations disrupted a meeting by stomping around, waving his arms, and ranting after a team member asked him a question he didn't think he should have to answer. You'd think he would have been stopped or asked to leave, but even the CEO (who was present at the time) didn't do anything to intervene.

Immediately following this particular meeting, the same vice president wrote a scathing, expletive-laden memo to the team. People found this incident quite disturbing, but sadly, no one knew how to deal with this situation. All it brought was paralysis.

As anxiety rises, people's ability to respond in a mature manner goes down. If you've ever witnessed a colleague undergo a complete breakdown over a minor setback or mistake, you know exactly what we're talking about. Many excellent employees, clients, and executives end up leaving companies after these types of childish incidents go unchallenged.

> ## *Encourage an adult exchange in all communication.*

Communication that is riddled with temper tantrums, lying, excuses, finger pointing, pouting, and personal attacks causes chaos. The only thing missing would be eating crayons during lunch.

Seven Ways to an Adult Learning Center

1. **Head them off at the pass.** We call this "stepping on their lines." When communicating, stay in the adult mode by being the announcer, not the color commentator. In this way, you encourage reporting of the facts. There is no good or bad news, just information. Encourage everyone to adopt a clear and mature language for working with each other.

   Specifically, eliminate the personal pronoun "you" during conflicts. "I" statements take responsibility for yourself; "you" statements puts blame on the other person.

2. **Translate all emotional commentary to more factual observations.** Edit all business communication for anger, exaggerations, righteous indignation, and criticism. Here is how the translation process works:
   - a). What do you know? (Observation)
   - b). Who is aware? (Accountability)
   - c). What do people want? (Expectation)
   - d). Who is responsible? (Commitment and closing the loop)

3. **Be direct.** This is where you describe what you believe is going on. Never attack a person; instead focus on the weakness in the strength of their position. For example, let's say you had a strong performer who was refusing to participate in a company meeting. His strength is his performance; the weakness in that strength is the example to the team.

4. **Ask questions.** Asking open-ended questions is a good way to help discover facts. Use questions to help people work through their emotions and opinions.

THE INCH PRINCIPLE ▨ 21 MILLION DOLLAR INCHES OF MANAGEMENT

5. Review-recap-remind. Instead of a knee-jerk reaction, try to review-recap-remind what you heard. This allows the other person to listen and hear what his comments sound like from your perspective. This also gives him the option to rephrase his words or rethink his position in a more productive manner.

6. Practice the art of negotiation. Successful managers define negotiations in the workplace as two parties having an adult conversation, each reserving the right to veto. There are only three positions management can take:

    • The first is to dictate and use their authority to keep the team in line.

    • The second is to let the employees call the shots and take advantage of the company.

    • The third is to negotiate. We encourage you to find ways to negotiate.

7. Encourage fair fighting. Childish behavior is easy to spot during conflict. Technology, especially, seems to have given people a "get out of jail free" card for hitting below the belt. In dirty fighting, there is just one simple rule—use any method to destroy your opponent.

Conversely, fair fighting is a form of conflict resolution reserved for adults who believe disagreement does not have to destroy. The rules of fair fighting are quite simple. Never lose control; keep the resolution focused on mutual gain, and refrain from the cheap shot.

Childish behavior will continue unless a strong leader encourages an adult learning center environment and then stands by it.

Graduate from a Day Care to an Adult Learning Center

Acting like grown-ups—in style. Temper tantrums—so last year.

When tension rises in the workplace, meltdowns become more common, and many managers find themselves running a day care center instead of an adult place of business.

You can trade in those day care sippy cups and time-outs by running an adult learning center instead. Refusing to allow tirades is your first order of business. After that, adult interaction is a simple case of making minor adjustments and helping employees to communicate appropriately and effectively.

Tear Up the Statement and Live the Mission

After reading our mission statement, I have to say it is one of the most idiotic things I have ever seen. I feel dumber for having read it. Management gets zero points for this effort.
- Employee

Remember mission statements that were all the rage? Executives swore by them. Employees swore at them. Take a few trite phrases about values, add some customer love, frame it on a wall in the lobby, and BAM! Greatness.

Mission statements are still around, of course. But now they're like frail celebrities at a cocktail party—important, sure, but everyone mostly ignores them.

Mission statements were supposed to DO something, to show us true north. But instead of words to live by, they were awkward, run-on sentences and flowery prose that were hard to follow and offered almost no relevance to our everyday activities.

How did this miracle management tool turn out to be such a fraud?

The first reason so many mission statements fail is that they are written for outsiders. In theory, they're meant to create a declaration that every employee in the organization can use to steer with, but in reality, the words are assembled to impress customers and investors. By the time the final draft is approved, the mission statement is really just a marketing tool.

Even the worst statement would probably be of some use if management held themselves and their teams accountable to it. But at some point, the gulf between the company's stated mission and its workplace reality simply becomes too wide. People can no longer make the connection.

> ## *The important part of a mission statement is the mission—not the statement.*

From time to time, I'll pay higher prices at the neighborhood national-chain supermarket, because the location is convenient. As I waited in the checkout line one day, I read the chain's corporate mission statement that was displayed on the wall. It read, in part: We will always strive to provide the best products at competitive prices.

Competitive prices? I pointed out to the young checker that I wasn't sure the store was living that part of its mission. She called the manager, and to his credit, he dismissed the sign as a "corporate thing." He explained that in reality, his store generally does have higher prices, but it offers greater variety, more specials, and easier checkout. I agreed with all of it—it was the mission they lived every day.

Why Wasn't It on the Sign?

The mission expressed by the store manager that day makes more sense than the one on the wall. It's more honest, to start with—it's also possible. Only in the sketchy world of advertising and marketing can you offer premium services at competitive prices.

> ## *Put your money where your mission is.*

Everyone knows how little it means when a company says, "We value our people," and then pays its employees as little as possible. How about the company who claims to "always put the customer first," but earns its profits by cutting corners on customer support and quality?

In the end, you're better off without a mission statement if you don't plan on living up to it. Today's employees are savvy. Goals, incentives, and clear expectations are far more effective than lofty mission statements.

THE INCH PRINCIPLE ■ 21 MILLION DOLLAR INCHES OF MANAGEMENT

Tear Up the Statement, and Live the Mission

A business' mission is work—it's not a Hallmark moment.

Give your employees a little credit; they know marketing hype when they see it, and they can distinguish between what's being sold to them by management and reality.

What employees need in order to connect to a company's expectations of them is simple: This is how our organization measures success. This is what we expect you to do to support the effort.

Anything less than this honest, straightforward approach will leave your team feeling duped—and doubting management's credibility. But a leader who lives by and rewards certain values and invests in something she believes in will convince her team that she's serious.

MILLION DOLLAR INCH

11

Make the Quickest Path to Success, the Quickest Path to Success

■ *I prefer not to set any goals. That way, I'm never disappointed.*

- Employee in hiding

Remember the fable of the tortoise and the hare? The rabbit dashed far ahead of the plodding shellback, stopped for a nap near the finish line, and overslept. The slow-and-steady turtle won the race, of course.

There's a lot to be said for moving people steadily along the path to success by setting goals they can reach with consistent effort. But then again, there's a lot to be said for the kind of bodacious goals that drive people and organizations to greatness.

No law says you can't have more than one kind of goal.

In your world, the tortoise and the hare are on the same team. Sometimes they're the same person. And if you're expected to win with both, it makes sense to adopt lines of communication (and goal setting) that appeal to both.

Some of your employees are home run hitters, but you do your company a disservice by only recognizing these efforts. By also rewarding consistent effort, you get the sort of momentum that builds on itself. Employees quit watching the clock. They become energized and enthusiastic about their work.

And before you know it, you've got a few new people swinging a bat in the on-deck circle and eyeballing that fence out there with the big white numbers on it.

Baseline and Brass Ring Goal Setting

Goal setting should have a baseline and a brass ring dimension. Baseline goals represent the acceptable minimum performance level, while brass ring represents exceptional personal achievement.

No one is going to set any records meeting the baseline. But you'd be surprised how much work gets done every day when people have goals they know they can meet.

> # *Get people used to succeeding, and you'll wind up with successful people.*

That's not to say there isn't a place for the brass ring effort, too. Reaching for growth and adding to what someone has already achieved makes the goals personal and keeps visionaries and glory-seekers interested.

But if brass ring is the only goal you have, the effort necessary to achieve it is nearly impossible to sustain on a consistent basis. People burn out. Or they hold back, knowing the extra effort will only result in a goal that's even higher. Once this happens, you'll have the devil's own time trying to get them to commit to the "new reality" plan you are pitching.

So What's the Answer?

One of our clients had a "Vision" retreat for shareholders only. At the retreat, they were told that the key to getting people excited is the ability to articulate an inspiring vision. Since we were working with the management team, they wanted ideas on how to "roll out" this vision to everyone. Their hope was to bring their teams together around a common goal. The goal was to grow their business and sell it for $35 million in fifteen years.

We suggested they give managers and employees a piece of the action. After we helped them up off the floor, they asked us if we had any other ideas!

We finally got them across the bridge of understanding that a "brass ring" goal; such as they were promoting, is always going to be a tough sell when the only people who benefit are the shareholders. No amount of cheerleading could make such a goal important to employees unless there was something in it for them—something besides ridiculously long hours and the absurd prospect of losing their jobs if they hit the goal. In the end, we advised our client to *set* the "brass ring" goal of selling the business at a large profit, but keep it private. Let's just call it our "crazy" goal. This way the ownership group could still feel excited about the goal, even though they chose not to share it openly with the teams.

Our next suggestion was to focus the work teams on realistic and achievable baseline goals that could be met every week. Momentum would take care of the rest.

Five years into the plan, we find our client slightly behind on their "crazy" goal. However, because of their baseline focus they are miles ahead of the competition.

With the downturn in the economy, came severe adjustments for the competition. Forced to admit publicly that the established goals were no longer realistic, they lost credibility with their work teams. Now they have the insurmountable task of selling a new goals program that includes cutbacks and layoffs.

When the economy went into recession, our client's front line people did not even notice. Their motivation and commitment has proceeded uninterrupted. Our client's message to their teams in this tough economy: *"Business as Usual"*.

In the current environment it may now take our client twenty years or longer instead of fifteen to meet their "crazy" goal, but they will make it. It seems our client's baselines became their company's lifeline.

Our client's experience is a reminder to hedge your bet. You don't need brass ring effort every week to hit a quarterly brass ring goal. You can do it with one or two brass ring weeks as long as you're getting baseline effort every week. And it's important to trade on that when you communicate your goals.

Make the Quickest Path to Success, the Quickest Path to Success

Setting goals is as much communication as motivation—and brass ring goals aren't the only ones worth reaching for.

Sure, you want your people to stretch for goals. But even more important, you want them to reach those objectives.

You can't get brass ring performance from anyone without his or her permission. So adding a clear baseline goal across the board will actually free your employees to take a swing at the sexier brass ring goals. Even when they miss, you still win—the baseline has been met, and they're eager to try again.

When you take your baseline goals seriously, you'll get consistent, week-to-week performance that builds skills, confidence, and ambition. And that gives you, the manager, the freedom to set bigger brass ring goals that drive growth and put money in everyone's pocket.

MILLION DOLLAR INCH

12

Memo to Everyone: Profit Is Not a Four-Letter Word

First place wins a trip to Hawaii. Second place is a gift certificate to Sizzler. And if you win third place, consider this your thirty-days' notice.

- Senior VP of sales

Most people have no idea how a business really operates. Everyone knows that certain numbers are important—if sales go up, so should profit, for example—but generally that's the extent of it.

Many progressive companies tend to overlook an underrated tactic for improving performance: teaching people the basics of business and how money is made and lost.

Still, should you spend time teaching employees how the company operates? The merits of open-book management are widely debated. Those in favor of it point to employee accountability and retention, and an improved bottom line. Others think it's just asking for trouble.

Even if you're not crazy about sharing sensitive financial information with your employees, it's still a good idea for them to know how business works. At the very least, they will begin to understand that the company owner's problems are their problems, too. And ultimately, profit is not something the owner steals from the workers, but a measure of each person's worth and value to the company.

Discuss the Facts of (Business) Life with Everyone

When she was in high school, my oldest daughter worked at our company for the summer. She did odd jobs in the office and ran occasional errands. One weekend I overheard her telling her mother about the deposit she had made at the bank that week.

"I can't believe how much money Dad makes," she said. That got my attention quickly! How to explain to her that there had barely been enough to get everyone paid?

"You think all of that money was mine?" I ventured. She was puzzled. "You own the company, don't you, Dad?" she responded.

Clearly, a little talk about the facts of business life was in order!

I used an analogy about a business owner who borrowed money to buy a large dinner table. This dinner table represented the corporation. When the corporation produced income, food appeared on the table. The bank slip my daughter had seen was an accounting of all of the "food" that appeared on our company's table that week. At the moment, it looked pretty full.

But the chairs around the table were for the dinner guests who would soon be joining the owner. Those "guests" are also known as expenses. I ran down the lengthy guest list, starting with Uncle Sam, his date the Bank, and of course, Patty Payroll.

"Everyone has to eat," I told my daughter. "If there are leftovers, the owner gets to keep them. But if the table runs short of food, the owner has to run to the store for more—and pay for it out of his own pocket."

But it can get worse. If things get really bad, some guests have to skip a meal—of course, never Uncle Sam or the Bank. And if that goes on long enough, the owner and all the guests—including Uncle Sam, the Bank, and Patty Payroll—have to find someplace else to dine. The Bank, I concluded for good measure, gets to keep the table.

"I guess you aren't as rich as I thought," my daughter finally said when my story was done.

> *This Million Dollar Inch is about making everyone—regardless of his or her position—aware of what's at stake, from an ownership perspective.*

Make It Their Problem, and They'll Do What Needs to Be Done

Another way to involve your employees in your company's success is to make the concerns of the business their concerns, and they'll do what needs to be done.

For starters, teaching your employees what keeps the business running will make it easier for them to swallow unpopular directives. But more importantly, they will begin to substitute their own self-interest where apathy and disregard for senior management problems once flourished.

In short, they will be more inclined to do what needs to be done—sometimes with spectacular results.

That's Not My Job!

My former partner was the owner of a security alarm company that grew from a one-man operation to six thousand clients and eighty employees in seven years. But it almost didn't happen.

Early on, my colleague was having trouble meeting payroll, even though sales were up. A closer analysis revealed that receivables were far higher than they should have been. His challenge to the senior management team to take responsibility for collections was met with blank stares and "not my job" grumbles. He then showed them the sales-to-collections ratio, and pointed out that unless things changed, some of the team would not be receiving a paycheck.

Suddenly, everyone was interested in the "owner's problem." Each manager took on delinquent accounts. The team effort resulted in a huge in-flux of receivables to the company.

Memo to Everyone: Profit Is Not a Four Letter Word

Bonuses and profit-sharing plans are a common way of rewarding employees for performance. So why not couple financial incentives with financial knowledge? The leader intent on leveraging such programs will find ways of explaining how the business actually operates—how money flows, where the choke points are, and how it affects everyone—from the president to the summer help.

Getting employees to think like owners can unleash a powerful bottom-line mentality throughout your organization. When employees really understand that profit is a good thing, you'll start to see more of it.

MILLION DOLLAR INCH

13

Manage Expectations with the Stages of Trust and Accountability

Success seems to be connected with action. Successful people keep moving. They make mistakes, but they don't quit.

- Conrad Hilton, Hilton Hotels

A minister, a Boy Scout, and a computer executive were the only passengers on a plane that was going down. Alas, the pilot announced, there were only three parachutes, but four people. He immediately claimed a parachute for himself, citing his responsibilities for a wife and three small children, and he jumped from the plane.

"I should have one, too," said the computer executive, "because I am the smartest man on the planet, and the world still needs me." He strapped the pack to his back and leaped from the plane.

The minister turned to the Boy Scout and said with a sad smile, "You are young, and I have lived a good life. You take the last parachute, and I'll go down with the plane."

"Relax, Reverend," said the Boy Scout. "The smartest man in the world just picked up my knapsack and jumped out of the plane." As the world's smartest man discovered, motivation without direction and communication often leads to failure. Conversely, giving clear direction and communication yields consistent success.

I'm a Little Bit Rock-n-Roll

I once worked for a telecom company that marketed electronic advertising directories for malls. During that time, I led a mall acquisition effort. Our most prominent potential client at the time was the Edward Debartolo family of shopping centers. Although I had failed for months to get an audience with Ed Debartolo, Jr., our board member Donny Osmond (yes, that Donny!) finally got him to agree to view a demonstration at one of his shopping centers. The pressure to perform was high.

The day before the demonstration, I stopped by to see how the installation was progressing. What I found was an angry mall manager, who told me that the workers had quit for the day! The contracted supervisor told me that their union required them to stop work at 5 p.m., and no amount of pressure could change it. I was in a bind; the job was not finished, and the Debartolo visit could not be moved.

A frantic call to our home office revealed the worst: we had no back-up plan to finish the job. The chief engineer told me that the only chance of the five directories becoming operational by the next morning was for me to step in and do the job myself.

You must understand, I am mechanically challenged. There are no calluses on these hands! But the chief engineer had confidence that I could do the job, and agreed to talk me through the tangle of cables, conduit, and satellite dishes.

The first two directories took hours, with the engineer instructing me step-by-step over the phone. As I started the third directory, he decided it was time for me to fly solo. "OK, Mr. Mechanical," he said. "Now you tell me how to do the next directory." I did my best.

As we finished the third directory, the engineer declared he was ready for a break. I, however, wanted to push ahead. We agreed that I would call if I had problems, and if not, I'd call when I finished the job.

It took me the balance of the night (and a few phone calls to the engineer), but by 7 a.m., I had performed a miracle. We were live for Mr. DeBartolo and Donny Osmond. I was dirty, tired, and my shirt was torn, but I had never felt better about an accomplishment. That day, I experienced growth, because the chief engineer led me through the stages of trust and accountability. If you're a manager who needs to delegate, you can expect to go through several stages of trust and accountability with your employees.

The Four Stages of Trust and Accountability

 Hands Off

You'll start with the **hands off** stage. The rallying cry of this level is, "It's not my job!" In fact, you actually want people to keep their hands off of certain things that truly are not their job. A few examples of things better left alone are safety features, lack of certification or qualification, and attention to low-level concerns that will cause you to miss a greater opportunity.

 Take Direction

At the **take direction** stage, employees will want to know, "What should I do?" Here, they will follow instructions and do as they are told. Make use of this tactic in the areas of new hires, people struggling in their jobs, personal problems that affect work, areas of significant opportunity, and when there is a need to get back to basics. In this stage, people are trainable and open to counsel and direction. But beware: managers and employees fail when their egos get in the way of asking for help or sharpening skills to stay competitive.

LEVEL 3 Training and Testing

You'll hear, "This is what I think we should do" when your employees enter the **training and testing** stage. Here, people are able to assess situations and provide recommendations to get the job done. Confidence grows as tasks are handled appropriately, and now is the time to give employees more freedom to develop their own ideas. Tools such as role-play, case studies, mentoring, cross-training, teamwork, and on-the-job observation provide many opportunities for people to show you that they are worthy of your trust.

LEVEL 4 Decision Making with a Return and Report Schedule

You've truly reached significant levels of trust and accountability when **decision making with a return and report schedule** becomes routine. Hearing, "This is what I just did" is Utopia for any manager. At this stage, employees are given plenty of scope and freedom to decide how to achieve the desired results. Typically, leaders of the teams are ready for responsibility and demonstrated their ability to make good decisions. If it's not critical that actions be approved beforehand, then "returning and reporting" decisions will allow for corrective action to be taken immediately if needed. Everyone needs to be accountable to someone.

I once had an assistant whom I trusted to streamline calls coming in to the office. Although I thought we were both clear on her job description, my struggle was with her accountability. In her mind, she was doing her job when she dutifully handed me a list of each person who called. And she was shocked when I gave her a less-than-stellar review.

It was obviously time for us to clarify what each of us expected. I expected her to take responsibility and make the effort to get my clients what they needed without my involvement. This would involve her renewed effort to relate to clients and learn our business. And she expected me to remember that she was not much of a mind reader! I'm happy to report that clarifying our expectations helped her to easily step into the role I had for her.

Effectively guiding people up and down the stages of trust and accountability is perhaps the single most powerful "high leverage" management activity there is. High leverage, in this case, is all about spending your time on activities that directly relate to achieving your personal and business goals.

This is a good opportunity to delegate responsibility to other skilled and higher-trained people so that you can focus your energies on other high leverage activities for which you are better suited.

If you've watched your business grow and develop in its early stages, you may find it difficult to let go, but choosing to delegate and assigning personal responsibility means growth for individual employees and for your business too.

THE INCH PRINCIPLE ■ 21 MILLION DOLLAR INCHES OF MANAGEMENT

Three Crucial Guidelines When Establishing Trust and Accountability

1. First, you can compress time frames, but you can't skip steps. It's OK for your people to fast-track the stages, as long as they don't take shortcuts to do it.

2. Second, if you have to bring someone down from the rafters of freedom, remember that he will feel like you took him apart. And if you take him apart, remember to put him back together.

3. Finally, there is no entitlement in the levels of trust and accountability. No one is "past that"... no one has "arrived."

Finally, don't forget that trust is the highest form of human motivation. It brings out the very best in people. But it takes time and patience, and it necessarily involves training and developing people so that their competency can rise to the level of trust you want to place in them.

Manage Expectations with the Stages of Trust and Accountability

This Million Dollar Inch will put manager and employee expectations on the same page.

For most people, growth is gradual and incremental. The goal is to recognize what stage you are in, and to move up or down a step as the situation warrants.

Beware, though, of skipping stages. This will widen the gap between your expectations and your employees' sense of entitlement. Comments from your team like, "I thought I was in charge?"..."That's not my job!"..."Since when do you expect that?"..."I don't need a baby-sitter!"...and of course, "I'm underpaid", will be clarified when your people know and understand the stages of trust and accountability.

MILLION
DOLLAR INCH

14

Beware of the Honor System

I already told you what I do all day. I work with people! My schedule is full of people stuff–isn't that obvious? I'm a people person–what's wrong with you people!

- Honor system employee describing his day

n the 1978 movie *The End*, Wendell Lawson had only six months to live. Suicide, he decided, was the way to go, but he failed at each attempt. In a final, desperate act, he drove to the California coast, determined to swim out into the ocean, where he would quickly tire and drown.

But the farther Wendell got from shore, the more he wanted to live. Though exhausted, he petitioned God for help back to the shore. "Oh, God!" he called out. "If I can just get back to shore, all that I have is yours!" He got a little closer to the shore and again called out, "Oh, God! If I make it, half of all I have is yours!" The approaching beach again had Wendell calling out, "Oh, God! Ten percent of all I have is yours if I can just live!"

He washed up on the beach, exhausted but alive. "Thank you, Lord!" he gasped. As he regained strength, he began to reconsider his bargain with the Almighty, and he finally convinced himself that the Lord didn't really deserve any credit for Wendell's safety. He rose to his feet, shook his fist at heaven, and shouted, "You have a lot of nerve trying to get my money!"

Sometimes you just can't win.

One of the biggest mistakes a manager can make is to give someone total autonomy when they are doing a great job.

It's easy to do. Why mess with success? Say you've got one person who finally gets it, and ten more that aren't quite there. Of course you're going to focus on the ten who are lagging and let the first one go out and knock 'em dead.

Or maybe you desperately need someone you can trust to operate on her own in some far-flung part of the organization. Maybe you just simply have top performers who deserve special treatment. One way or another, you'll eventually find yourself putting someone on the honor system.

You should think twice about it.

It's human nature to grant autonomy to someone who has proven his loyalty to the company and his ability to succeed with minimal supervision. But just ask Wendell Lawson how easy it is to forget where you come from. In the honor system, people are given freedom to govern themselves, and trusted not to take unfair advantage of the situation.

You can see the risks inherent in that simple description of granting honor. Yet most managers refuse to consider them. They believe that granting such trust is the highest reward they may bestow on a valued member of their team. And much of the time, that's true. Trust is the highest form of human motivation. But problems—and risks— arise when the assignment is open-ended and there is no accountability attached to the deal.

> ## When people are out of sight, they tend to go out of mind.

I once worked for the home office of a national company. In my role, I had to shut down our best branch and let everyone go on the spot—including our former "Manager of the Year."

Turns out, the entire office had been freelancing with the manager's permission. No one in the home office had any idea until our CEO was tipped off. Later, the ex-manager seemed genuinely sorry, and told me he wasn't even sure how he had managed to let things get out of hand.

It was clear to me what had happened, and not all of it was his fault. As a reward for excellent performance, this former Manager of the Year had been given too much authority and far too little accountability.

People, left on their own, have a natural tendency to distance themselves from the reality of their situation. They believe they have arrived solely on their own merits; and they forget how much time, money, and support the company has invested in their success. They talk themselves into believing that management is unaware of their individual accomplishments, or chooses not to recognize them.

THE INCH PRINCIPLE ■ 21 MILLION DOLLAR INCHES OF MANAGEMENT

And from there, it's just a short step for the employee to believe he is justified in finding ways to reward himself, in proving his worth by defecting to a competitor, or in living on the inheritance of his past success.

In extreme cases, the consequences can be disastrous. Have you seen the movie *Apocalypse Now*? Deep in the jungle, cut off from his command structure, a U.S. military commander goes insane with power, forms his own army, and sets himself up as a god to the local natives. Of course, he had to be terminated "with extreme prejudice."

Hopefully this won't happen to you, but it's still worth remembering that you aren't doing your people any favors by leaving them on their own. Successful people need accountability as much as the company does.

By submitting to this accountability, employees who have demonstrated good judgment are given the freedom to exercise it in whatever way they

> *Permit freedom, but require accountability.*

see fit. How that accounting is handled offers opportunities for both employee and employer to either build on the trust or retreat from it in a responsible way, while minimizing risk to the company.

Beware of the Honor System

A good leader understands the psychology of ambition—how to cultivate it and when to restrain it. Ambitious people almost always think they can do things better than the current process, and they will pay dearly for the chance to try. It's often this lack of opportunity that provokes some people to jump ship or strikeout on their own, sometimes taking millions of dollars worth of ideas with them.

Being able to strike the right tone with people who crave the honor system holds tremendous potential value in all areas of your organization, but you have to have patience, awareness, and strong lines of communication.

A major part of that communication is passing on the certain knowledge that freedom will be accompanied by accountability. So, beware of trading accountability for promises—or risk the disastrous consequences.

MILLION DOLLAR INCH

15

Establish a Red Zone to Protect the Company

Always protect the mission by getting permission from a high authority to take a high-risk action.

- *Major General, U.S. Marine Corps*

magine a small engine room in the middle of your organization's building. In the room is a closely protected object. It could be any object, really, but it represents the core power responsible for your company's continued success. And next to the priceless object is a case of dynamite with an explosion cable that runs out under the door and beyond—right to the heart of your company's everyday activity. It's not as far-fetched as it sounds. Every organization—indeed, every management career—contains the seeds of its own destruction.

And those "seeds of destruction" start with people. They do unexpected things. They're good at hiding their personal problems at work, but can't seem to keep those same stresses and motivations out of their decision-making. And when their decisions become suspect, they can be quite persuasive or even dishonest in their own defense.

In short, when things blow up, the chain of cause-and-effect is often hard to believe after the fact, and nearly impossible to see ahead of time.

> *Realistically, there's nothing you can do about the dynamite. But wouldn't it be nice to know when that fuse was lit?*

Part of being (and remaining!) a successful leader means being alert to the signs that someone's performance, behavior, or situation has become a liability to the organization. We like to call these signs the "Red Zone." It's a warning area, like a moat, that surrounds the entrance to your metaphorical room. When breached, the alarm goes off, and it's time for management to execute emergency procedures.

There Are No Gray Areas in the Red Zone

How does an employee enter the Red Zone? Beware when most or all of his skills, knowledge, attitude, drive, and commitment fall below your baseline expectations. A salesperson missing his quota is one thing. But if that salesperson then refuses to attend training, blames outside circumstances, and won't make calls, he has entered the Red Zone. Watch out for blatant disregard for safety guidelines, carelessness, and an "I don't care" attitude too; companies lose millions of dollars each year by not handling Red Zone situations in a timely and appropriate way.

Don't fool yourself into thinking that you can skirt around these Red Zone issues in a way that avoids unpleasant confrontation. It's just wishful thinking. True, you won't always know exactly what went wrong from the very beginning, but that's not the point. Managing in the Red Zone requires you to presume the worst to protect the company. Your company's procedures already in place are designed to assess and mitigate the situation. The time for interpretation has past.

Fire in the Oil Tank!

If you're still not convinced, consider the story I was told about a military aircraft pilot trainee. Like all trainees, he had to memorize all emergency procedures without a lot of explanation. One procedure puzzled him: when the hydraulic overheat warning light came on, he was to idle the engine immediately. If the warning light remained lit after thirty seconds, he was to eject!

This seemed rash. If a "check engine" light comes on in a car, the engine still runs…and he was supposed to ditch a five-million dollar aircraft? He went to an experienced aircraft hydraulics mechanic for the answer.

"The hydraulics system is connected to the jet's engine," the mechanic explained. "The turbine turns, the shaft turns, and the pump turns, which build pressure in the system."

He went on to explain the oil reserve tank and the sensor that sticks into it, activating the red light when the temperature inside the tank exceeded 278° F. If the light remains red even after all new pressure is shut down, there are only two possible explanations: the sensor has malfunctioned, or there's a fire in the oil tank.

Suddenly, ejecting didn't seem like such a bad idea.

THE INCH PRINCIPLE ■ 21 MILLION DOLLAR INCHES OF MANAGEMENT

In the same way, the Red Zone lets you know when someone's performance has become a liability to the company. It might be a simple misunderstanding, but you still have a fire in the oil tank. That's why certain behaviors like sexual harassment, discrimination, retaliation, intimidation, and theft are automatic Red Zone incursions—even when they aren't accompanied by sub-par performance.

Stranger Danger!

A successful senior manager I know told me how his handling of a sensitive situation put his entire company at risk and earned him a demotion. He was a motivator, a coach to a team that worked hard, played hard, and shared one another's successes.

So when word got out that two of his team members were having an affair, the rest of the team didn't see it as a threat. The affair was discreet, and it didn't affect the team's performance. "We're all adults here" was the prevailing attitude.

That all changed one day—or should have—when the woman met with the manager and confessed. She told him that she planned to break off the illicit relationship and try to patch things up with her husband. She turned down the manager's offer to help if there were any problems.

Never mind the employee—the manager should have been asking the company's legal counsel what action he should take instead. Sexual harassment in the workplace is an automatic Red Zone situation, and that includes any behavior that can possibly be construed as sexual in content. His second mistake was not taking any notes or notifying someone else of the meeting and its substance.

Three months later, without warning, the woman resigned and filed a sexual harassment lawsuit against the company. In the suit, she claimed that she had disclosed the matter to her immediate supervisor, who "didn't do anything."

This is one of those times when you face the music and go by the book.

THE INCH PRINCIPLE ▣ 21 MILLION DOLLAR INCHES OF MANAGEMENT

There are usually—but not always—reasonable explanations for unacceptable behavior in the workplace, and there are other courses of action available besides termination. Nevertheless, a Red Zone situation means it's time to face the music and bring immediate, by-the-book confrontation. That's why "the book" exists.

- Always go to the proper authority with a plan for improving performance. Cite specific examples of the unacceptable behavior. Identify and make available appropriate support and resources for improvement. Communicate the means by which improvement will be measured. Specify consequences if improvement does not occur.

- Apply progressive discipline, ranging from verbal and written reprimands escalating to a number of days suspension from work.

- Reassign the employee to a different skill level, manager, department, or team.

- Terminate the employee immediately, if the situation warrants, or as a result of noncompliance in the areas listed above.

The manager's response must be direct, consistent, and seen as a clear protection of the company's interests.

Always create a paper trail and get advice from human resources and/or the legal department in order to validate your approach.

THE INCH PRINCIPLE ■ 21 MILLION DOLLAR INCHES OF MANAGEMENT

Establish a Red Zone to Protect the Company

The financial impact of sub-par performance on your company can range from significant to staggering.

Small decisions lead to losses that tend to multiply when people cover up, sugarcoat, or otherwise refuse to mitigate their behavior. The ensuing costs of refunds, recalls, and legal defense can drive an organization to the brink of bankruptcy and beyond. Add in punitive damages or criminal convictions, and your company may be facing a situation from which it can never recover.

While it's easy to blame a litigious society for the proliferation of complaints, employers need only look in the mirror to find the root cause.

Most formal employment-related charges escalate because management can't be trusted to be fair or to do the right thing. It's your responsibility to protect the company—and your employees—by creating a workplace that is free of liability and run by executives, managers, and supervisors (the target of most complaints) who are trained to deal with poor performance.

Always Work to Bring Them Back From BOHICA

☐ *David:* If you don't turn this Michael McDonald CD
   that you've been playing for two years
   straight off, I'm going to kill everyone in
   the store and put a bullet in my brain.

Paula: David, what do you suggest we play?

David: I don't care. Anything. I would rather watch
   "Beautician and the Beast." I would rather
   listen to Fran Drescher for eight hours than
   have to listen to Michael McDonald.
   Nothing against him, but if I hear "Yah Mo
   B there" one more time, I'm going to "Yah
   Mo" burn this place to the ground.

- 40 Year Old Virgin

BOHICA (acronym, n.):

Bend Over, Here It Comes Again; characterized by experienced, cynical employees ("Bohicans") with long memories, misused and unappreciated talents, and signs of brilliance; often productive, but prone to bouts of unhappiness and dissatisfaction with themselves, others, and their situations.

(Term coined by professor of organizational development Dick Dunsing.)

Know any Bohicans? If you work in the business world, you do! They don't just work with you. They have their own village.

BOHICA Village is a talented but troubled area. Its residents are under-appreciated, they've gotten a raw deal, and, well, life is unfair. Used to be, an attitude like that could get you fired. It didn't matter if you knew more than the boss did or you could hit your goals in your sleep. Complaining, slacking off, and bad-mouthing your betters bought you a one-way ticket to the unemployment line.

But companies can't afford to fire their Bohicans today, because there's too much talent and productivity worth saving behind those village walls. The problem is getting to it.

> ## There's a lot of value locked up in BOHICA Village—if you can just get to it.

People go to BOHICA for a lot of reasons. Day trips are as common as rain—you have a bad day or you lose a deal or miss a goal, and you might as well pack your duffel for a trip to the village. Nearly everyone spends a night or two there at some point.

But it's a different story when one of your people settles in to BOHICA for an extended stay. When a company has an employee in BOHICA, it fails to get a return on it's investment. Worse, the rest of your team is be-ing exposed to a corrosive opportunity. And the longer an employee stays in BOHICA Village, the more it costs in lost time and missed opportuni-ties. Most dangerous of all, he'll invite others to visit.

There will almost always be a great deal of drama when you stage a rescue mission on behalf of your wayward Bohican. Personal and policy issues, broken promises, and lack of respect are all lurking just below the surface—and sometimes not even that deep. In most cases, long-time residents have traded in a mature view of things for schoolyard compari-sons. Their scrambled priorities make mountains out of molehills, and "straw man" complaints over petty issues.

This was clearly the case with a talented man we met who was not only a year-round resident of BOHICA Village, but was apparently running for mayor, too.

He was one of his company's top performers, even as he ran down the organization to anyone who would listen, including junior employees and customers. He was about to be reprimanded when we learned the source of his unhappiness. Apparently, he had been written up for taking too many breaks. He told us he "knew for a fact" that the office receptionist was taking extra breaks on a regular basis and was "getting away with it."

We listened to him gripe for a while, and then asked him a simple question: "When you consider the discrepancy in pay, whom should be the better example of dedication to the company? A top performer or a part-time receptionist?"

This long-term resident and future mayor of BOHICA Village started to look uncomfortable. He finally mumbled, "Maybe I should quit compar-ing my situation to hers." A reminder that to whom much is given, much is required finally convinced him to pack his bags and head back from the village.

> # *Reclaiming someone from BOHICA Village is basically a rescue mission.*

Applying this Million Dollar Inch helps you realize a couple of things as a leader.

First, most people are on their way to or from the village. It's a condition. And treatment can be as simple as having a private word in the hall, or as complex as renewing someone's sense of leadership.

Second, you'll begin to see that some members of your management team are better suited to rescuing wayward Bohicans than others. Use them.

Third, what gets rewarded gets done. Status, compensation, recognition, and commitment are all common topics in BOHICA Village.

As you plan your strategy, remember that the best communication strategy is to discuss someone's leadership abilities or potential. Never discuss someone's attitude—instead, ask if his behavior reflects leadership. Anyone who has talent and can perform his job is a leader. Let him decide if he's willing to step up and take a leadership role, or if things are as good as they are going to get.

Finally, as you attempt to bring your Bohicans back from the village, it's vital that you lower your expectations. In the village, movement equals improvement. People must decide for themselves to move out of the neighborhood.

Bohicans won't generally leave the village by themselves. You actually have to go and get them, and when you do, keep conversations private, offline, and informal. Make sure you separate performance from behavior—it's the behavior you want to adjust. Ask your grumbling team member to show some leadership by agreeing to pass his negatives up to you, rather than down to the rest of the organization. Skip the ultimatums (for now), and give your Bohican a chance to self-correct. In the long run, it's best for the entire team.

Always Work to Bring Them Back From BOHICA

Many of your employees have knowledge and skills that are being held hostage by a lack of desire to perform. But what would it mean if you could reclaim all of that pent-up productivity and replace a malcontent with a champion?

That's what freeing residents of BOHICA Village is all about.

A successful business leader understands the potential value of human capital and the leverage each person holds over it. Discontent, complaints, and bad attitudes in otherwise talented people are often a case of twisted pride. Give your Bohicans a way out of their own dilemma, and you just may get a lot of that pride back on your side.

#17

Spend Quality Time with Your Quality People

> We live in a fast-paced world. If you don't take time with your best people, you might wake up and find they have moved on.

> - Production Manager

Have you ever been surprised when your best person quit?

It's a trick question. If you said yes, then you weren't paying attention. If you said no, then you didn't know how to keep that valued team member. And if you said, "My good people never leave," then you're either lying or you run a cult.

Since there's really no good answer to this question, let's instead use it to focus attention on something managers often neglect or misunderstand, at great cost to the organization: dealing successfully with successful people.

When someone is successful, it's tempting to leave well enough alone. Why mess with a good thing, right?

Wrong.

If you don't devote some quality time to your quality people, you'll eventually find yourself at their mercy, one way or another. We've seen how this happens with the "honor" system (a.k.a., deliberately staying out of touch). If you swing too far the other way and parade someone's every accomplishment before the entire organization, she'll start to buy into her own hype and eventually hold you hostage to her salary demands or attitudes.

> ## You can't take top performers for granted—but you can't let them hold you hostage either.

Successful people are empowered and often are stubborn on the subject of their own worth. But some managers have a knack for reminding star players that success is not a one-sided relationship. Bill Belichick, head coach of the NFL's New England Patriots, is one.

Halfway through their record-breaking 2007 season, the Patriots were beating their opponents by an average of more than four touchdowns. Reporters asked the players over and over how they were able to stay focused. The answer: Coach Belichick's pride-busting approach to handling stress.

Early each week, Coach Belichick exposed the various individual lapses that occurred, no matter how lopsided the victory. And he singled out the star players first. This came to be known as "Humble Pie." At one point in the season, the entire team showed up wearing "Humble Pie—I Eat It" t-shirts. Coach Belichick's said "Humble Pie—I Serve It."

By definition, successful players are also the ones who leave at the top of their games. In professional sports, that often means retirement. Business people who are at the top of their games usually get stolen by a competitor. It's a fact of business life: top people get recruited. Sometimes offers are just too good to turn down. But it's important for senior managers to understand that key employees hardly ever wake up one day and decide to leave.

Watch out! Once your employee starts systematically exploring other options, his chances of jumping ship go up significantly. The grass is looking greener. If management remains unaware or uncommunicative about the situation, it will be perceived as taking the employee's loyalty for granted. The decision to leave becomes that much easier.

It costs you nothing to find out what motivates your top employees.

Find out what it takes to lose your best people...

Talking about those things will usually yield areas of mutual benefit, such as wider-ranging interests, different venues, or the desire for more challenging assignments that are likely to increase the return to the company with very little additional investment or disruption.

The nice thing about "quality time" is that it doesn't have to take much actual time. These people get it. You can be honest. And you can (and must) hold them accountable.

THE INCH PRINCIPLE ▪ 21 MILLION DOLLAR INCHES OF MANAGEMENT

But keep these touches regular; it's the only way you'll know what's going on with your best employees, and it's an excellent way to find out what needs changing or fixing. It's also the only credible way to serve up the occasional humble pie.

When you look for ways to develop people, enhance the workplace and maximize opportunities for people to stay, you not only get an immediate return of hard work and appreciation—you're improving your company too. You're setting a tone that encourages future strivers. You're increasing the length of time that your best people will stay, and during that time, the company gets the most from them.

Four Ways to Develop Your People

1. Recognize and Reward

Recognition is nutrition for the soul. But it's not in limited supply, and it's not reserved just for those who need motivating. Everyone needs it—particularly those who are doing the best jobs.

Like accountability, recognition is confirmation for your top people that they are expending their considerable talents on the right work. In the absence of recognition and reward, some people are self-motivated. But that's a silly reason to withhold it.

> *Recognition is nutrition for the soul.*

While you're recognizing performance, make a special effort to single out those who support your star employees too. They are the ones who enable success, and they know it. Publicly, they tend to deflect such recognition to the rest of their team. Privately, it makes them whole. Cash compensation always motivates. But never underestimate the power of individual recognition and direct praise when it's based on job performance.

2. Raise the Bar

Counter intuitive as it may seem, adding demanding tasks to the workload tends to stoke the effort of peak producers. By offering more challenging assignments, you are letting valued employees know that you appreciate what they are doing and trust them to handle more responsibility. At the same time, raising the quality and importance of the work they do justifies the high level of trust you already have in them.

Raising the bar accomplishes at least three positive things.

First, it helps you avoid the temptation to put top employees on the honor system where they are out of touch. Second, it creates a proving ground that positions your best people for promotion (should they excel) or for improvement (should they not). Finally, it ties top employees, their work, and their business relationships closer to the strategic plans of the company—a move that directly counters their possible defection.

3. Improve Their Market Value

Investing in an employee's career development works hand-in-hand with raising the bar. People operating at the top of their game can especially benefit from training and personal mentoring, particularly if new responsibilities carry them into uncharted territory.

Improving market value is an efficient use of career development dollars, as talented people are far more likely to learn well and apply what they learn immediately in their own self-interest. Increasing a top employee's marketability almost always produces a return of hard work and appreciation in the near term. Beyond that, managers should constantly be on the lookout for ways to enhance the workplace and maximize opportunities for their best people to pad their résumés by staying with the company, rather than leaving.

4. Get-Out-of-Jail-Free Passes

One of your most effective management tools is the discretion to make other people's lives a little easier.

THE INCH PRINCIPLE ▪ 21 MILLION DOLLAR INCHES OF MANAGEMENT

A half-day or a long weekend off means a lot to today's time-pressured families. Early getaways on the eve of holidays are especially welcome. Your top people have earned some consideration when it comes to flexible hours or telecommuting privileges. Passes can also take the form of guilt-free opportunities to opt out of certain less-desirable activities, meetings, or paperwork. Be judicious and always give the pass a context.

Managers who fail to reward quality performance with quality attention will lose good people for the wrong reasons. On the other hand, offering recognition rewards and trust with accountability inspires leadership in others and can help them reach levels of performance they would not reach on their own.

Spend Quality Time with Your Quality People

Every manager knows that it costs far more to replace an effective employee than to do what it takes to keep him. So why is retaining valuable people such an under-utilized skill?

Successful companies—and those who lead them—understand that employee retention programs may be the best long-term investment they can make.

It begins with an attitude. It's taking care of loyal employees who display the knowledge, skills, and desire to succeed. It's not only the right thing to do, but it's the financially smart thing to do.

How much additional profit might the company earn by applying innovative ideas from people who already work for you? How much could it save by avoiding expensive, disruptive regime change and instituting practical, necessary change from within instead?

Taking care of your top people means more than paying them well. It means using them to build the future of your company by knowing what will drive them away.

Encourage New People to Give Up Their Right to Fail

Go into a job with your eyes and ears open and eager to learn. Remember that everyone has something to teach you on a new job and it is important to allow others to share their experiences and knowledge. And finally, if you do not know the answer – do not be afraid to say so but then be willing to pursue the answer and learn from the experience.

- Hiring Manager

S tatistics tell us that the next ten years will be an employee-driven market, because of a whole host of issues, from boomers leaving the workforce to future generation's lack of interest in working for someone else. A shortage of skilled and talented workers is a major concern.

Federal labor statistics show that workers in almost every age group are staying at jobs for a shorter period of time. The numbers reflect a change in people's attitudes about their careers and changing jobs. The days are gone when many people could expect to stay at a single company, moving steadily up the ladder and then retiring.

Today, more employees—especially those under 30—view themselves as "free agents" who must actively manage their own careers. They realize their companies may lay them off at any moment. They know their economic survival depends on maintaining cutting-edge skills. And so they don't feel a drop of guilt about jumping ship if another job offers better pay or more growth opportunity.

So, where does this leave those of us in management? Is it a waste of time and money to train these "free agents"? Should we ignore them? If we do, time and money is lost cleaning up the mess untrained people leave behind.

Sometimes you just have to step back from the conventional wisdom and see what common sense has to say about it. In this case, common sense is scratching its head over the idea that not training people who *might* jump ship at a better opportunity and allowing them to fail is good business.

What does a person who has no idea what they're doing in the first place learn from that?

In fact, the opposite is true. New hires are the very ones who must give up their right to fail. They are in learning mode. They are fresh, open-minded, teachable, willing to submit, and ready to believe that management has their best interests at heart. Lord knows it won't last, so this is your window of opportunity to imprint them with the culture, methods, and common language of your company. It's the time to teach success, identify land mines, and clearly communicate both management expectations and employee entitlements.

Inexperience isn't the only qualification for being on a short leash. Successful employees get promoted into unfamiliar environments all the time. It makes no sense for the company to reward someone with new pressures and responsibilities, then leave him alone to fall on his sword— or worse, to fail on an important assignment—because he lacks specific knowledge or skills.

In the movie *City Slickers*, advertising executive Mitch Robbins hits a bad patch and concludes that his job amounts to nothing more than selling air—actual air. With his most recent commercial a failure, his boss finally forces Mitch to run all ads past him until he gets back on track. Even seasoned veterans occasionally hit the wall or go into a prolonged slump. At some point, they too must give up the right to fail and allow themselves to be watched and helped until they regain their confidence or relearn what they had done so well before.

> ## *The right to fail must be earned.*

If there is such a thing as the right to fail, it has to be earned. There are good reasons for this. Failure—or lack of success—is an outcome that must be kept in perspective if it is to be of any use at all.

Employees have to know the rules in order to break them on purpose. They have to understand the process before they can get creative.

Failure has an unpredictable effect on people new to their jobs. They don't know enough to know how or why things turned out badly. Some will assume the worst about their own performances and completely overreact. Such crises of confidence are out of proportion with events and can color a person's decision making for years to come.

THE INCH PRINCIPLE ■ 21 MILLION DOLLAR INCHES OF MANAGEMENT

Even more annoying are those who do not see a negative outcome as a failure, but rather as an opportunity to fix the company. A lack of constraints in this case has reinforced the person's notions of his or her own inherent talent. Such attitudes can be difficult to dislodge and make the people who hold to them effectively unteachable.

New people will learn from their mistakes, if management has the good sense to create and maintain a short-term, low-risk environment in which learning is the sole requirement and the impact of mistakes is minimized.

Ninety-Day Game Plan for Greatness Defined

Having a game plan for the first ninety days is essential. It should be intense enough to keep trainees busy at all times, but flexible enough to compress time frames without skipping steps for experienced people.

Orientation is to welcome, inform, and integrate. Don't make employees learn these things the hard way!

The Classroom is the setting for people to listen, take notes, do home-work, and pass tests—just like school. The classroom is where students become humble and teachable, where they learn your common language. No one skips class, regardless of "experience." Everyone starts at square one and learns to do things your way.

Scavenger Hunt is giving your new people a list of items with where to find them. This allows new people to learn without having to be attached to your hip the whole time. You may have them work with different people, research information or be a "fly on the wall" with different departments.

A Risk-Free Environment will improve performance through case studies, role play, and game situations that will help inexperienced people practice basic skills, and veterans to scrape off the rust.

Observation and Coaching take one of two forms. In the first, trainees observe skilled trainers doing the work—it's the watch-and-learn method. Here, they will have a checklist of observations and will have the chance to ask questions and be tested. In the other form, a coach observes trainees doing their work and critiques the effort.

Picking Your Winners Too Early is an easy-to-make mistake. True, competition breeds competence, but don't write off the slow starts. Not all successful people are quick studies. In a franchise training program I ran years ago, one would-be owner stood out for his lack of confidence and seeming inability to retain the material. He even had to repeat the program with another group. My staff figured this person would last six months, tops. Today, out of 230 offices, his is in the top five in production. When the founder of the organization passed away, this owner received the inaugural Founder's Award for the franchisee who best represented the founder's principles for success.

Compressing Time Frames is fine, but skipping steps is not. When you consider the wide variety of candidates for training, it's tempting to take short cuts, particularly for "experienced" people. Be careful with this. Some people will come to you with ten years' experience; others have one year of experience, repeated ten times.

Assigning Mentors will lead to smoother operating functions, lower turnover, and better employee satisfaction. The role of a mentor can be as simple as a once-a-week lunch to show new hires the ropes and to pass on some of the unwritten corporate culture that is rarely acknowledged in formal training settings.

With your new hire game plan in place, you'll be certain that new employees are getting a base of knowledge that's consistent with management's expectations.

THE INCH PRINCIPLE ▓ 21 MILLION DOLLAR INCHES OF MANAGEMENT

Encourage New People to Give Up Their Right to Fail

Some of the world's most respected business leaders spend a surprising amount of time with new recruits. If the pace of business is so hectic, why would they bother?

That hectic pace is the very reason it's important to make such an impression on new hires. There's no time for extended periods of orientation and "settling in." There's no time to let people fail or to allow them a second chance to make a first impression. These companies know the extraordinary value of getting new people off on the right foot.

Communicating a sense of urgency and connecting top leadership with the greenest employees is a quick way to instill trust, continuity, and confidence in management and in the processes these new team members are expected to learn. What results is a serious view of training and a successful start for the people who could contribute so much to your company's success.

Close the Monkey Adoption Agency

There are two kinds of people, those who do the work, and those who take the credit. Try to be in the first group; there is less competition there.

- Indira Gandhi

M anagement is a lightning rod for monkeys—not the dirty, scratchy kind...worse.

In the classic "Who's Got the Monkey?" article in the Harvard Business Review (1974), authors William Oncken and Donald Wass tell the tale of an overburdened manager who allows others to leave their problems and responsibilities at his doorstep. With each "monkey" that leapt from someone's back to his own, the manager's Monkey Adoption Agency got more overcrowded. He lost control of his schedule and struggled to keep responsibility where it belonged. Overloaded with monkeys, the manager failed to develop his team effectively.

Oncken and Wass could never have imagined the speed at which today's supersonic monkeys are transferred with the aid of technology.

Let's Slow Down a Typical "Monkey" Transfer

• The monkey has an owner and home base.
  "I have a problem or concern."

• Manager and monkey-owner interact.
  "You have new messages in your in-box."

• The manager feeling pressure opens the adoption agency.
  "How can I help?"

• The responsible party transfers the monkey.
  "I need you to bail me out."

• The manager officially adopts the Monkey.
  "Where is all this pressure coming from?"

Monkey Adoption 101

When you check your e-mail, sit in a meeting or take a call with someone, think about if it ends with you saying any of the following:

- **- I got it!**
- **- Let me review your situation!**
- **- My door is always open!**
- **- I'll work on this at home tonight!**
- **- Let me think about that!**
- **- I can help you with that!**
- **- Don't worry about it, I'll take care of it (or I'll handle it.)**
- **- If you have problems, just let me know.**
- **- If you can't do it I'll figure out how to get it done.**
- **- You don't have time? OK, well I can do this for you.**
- **- I'll find someone to do it for you.**
- **- I understand!**
- **- Don't worry about it!**

If these sound familiar, then you are most likely adopting a bunch of monkeys. When you do this, you are acting out of a sense of loyalty and concern. However, this prevents other people from taking personal responsibility and brings the learning curve to a screeching halt.

How Can Management Be Helpful, without Adopting?

A simple way of making sure you only take monkeys with your name on them (and keep the doors of the adoption agency barred) is to deflect responsibility to where it belongs. A manager's e-mail, voice mail, and other interactions are fraught with opportunities to increase the number of poor orphan monkeys in his or her care. We all know that if you touch it, you own it. A manager at a robotics company was so sick of his eighty e-mails a day that his only recourse was "shift, page down, delete." That approach was just as ineffective as running the adoption agency.

THE INCH PRINCIPLE ▦ 21 MILLION DOLLAR INCHES OF MANAGEMENT

153

> ## Keep responsibility where it belongs!

Deflection is a safe and sane way to keep monkeys at bay. They'll try to slip past you disguised as questions, comments, statements, emotional outbursts, "if-looks-could-kill" and other nonverbal signals, and verbal attacks.

Get ready to defend and protect yourself—those monkeys will fly at you, and you must send them back to where they belong.

Five Questions to Deflect the Monkeys

Here are five questions that allow you, in a professional manner, to do a paternity test to determine who truly owns a monkey.

1. What's on your mind?

2. What were you hoping for?

3. What are the options?

4. If you were me, how would you answer that?

5. If I agree, what can I expect in return?

It's every manager's job to take charge and direct the monkey traffic. Don't bother waiting for others to recognize their irresponsible actions. If you're afraid to deflect a monkey because it has "special needs," then create a joint custody arrangement with the owner. Adopting monkeys and allowing the owner to be an absentee parent is ineffective. In fact, many times, the responsible manager gets the blame when things do not work out.

Let's Get Excited!

In the early 80s, I found myself between jobs. I picked up the want ads, looking for the opportunity of a lifetime. This one caught my eye: "Your last career stop! Call for a personal interview."

How could I say no? I showed up the next day, and settled in as the lights went down, the lasers started flashing, and the company spokesperson bounded onto the stage.

He outlined the company's history and the innovative products that had taken them to Fortune 1000 status. "As we expand our product line," he announced, "we're looking for the next generation of millionaires!" Those who were interested were invited to come back the next day.

I was the first person back the next morning, and I was surprised that I was one of only a few to return. I was ushered in where I was ambushed with information about this innovative product, this last career stop. My job would be—you guessed it—selling vacuum cleaners door-to-door.

I lunged for the exit, but came up short. The manager who broke my fall said, "Don't judge us too early. It's my job to motivate you to be success-ful." I was invited to spend a day with him and his team in the field—an offer I accepted.

The next morning we were all set to begin a day of canvassing the neighborhood. The manager then trotted out one of his motivation techniques. We all stood in a circle, our hands almost touching, while the manager slipped a cassette into a giant boom box (it was the '80s!). The song of choice: "I'm So Excited," made famous by the Pointer Sisters. This version, however, had been modified for the industry: "I'm so excited!" it screamed. "About selling vacuums!"

All of the men erupted into a chorus of euphoria. There were high fives all around, and an excitement approaching religious zeal over vacuums as we hit the street.

THE INCH PRINCIPLE ▦ 21 MILLION DOLLAR INCHES OF MANAGEMENT

155

But the manager's efforts were short-lived. After a barrage of rejection, all of that motivation and energy evaporated. The salespeople were talking negative, complaining, and appeared lethargic.

The monkey it seems was 100 percent on the back of this dedicated manager. The manager heaped all the pressure on himself and his motivational bag of tricks to get his team to perform. It wasn't long before we all called it quits and many blamed the manager for their lack of success.

Learning to deflect monkeys and negotiate joint custody arrangements is a strong leadership skill. It takes effort and energy, but it's worth it to develop employee involvement. It's worth it to help employees succeed, and meet expectations. You build the employee's self-confidence, and people who feel successful usually are successful.

Close the Monkey Adoption Agency

People are philanthropic when it comes to a leader's time and energy! They assume you won't mind caring for their problematic monkeys in your very own Monkey Adoption Agency. Monkeys are a metaphor for taking the lead on tasks and responsibilities. Monkeys live on people's backs and they can be exchanged and moved around from person to person. Refusing to accept challenges that people try to delegate upward, and instead giving them opportunities to take responsibility for the care and feeding of their monkey is the best choice for both the monkey and for its keeper. The person who is closest to the challenge usually has the knowledge and skill to solve the problem, if allowed to do so.

So protect yourself! The simplest method you can use is deflection. Use it to thin the herd, or to determine a monkey's paternity. Placing a monkey with its rightful owner will allow you to be involved in deeper issues, such as getting organized, delegating, planning, and investing time with key personnel.

Declare the Monkey Adoption Agency closed!

MILLION DOLLAR INCH

#20

Name that Meeting

A meeting is an event where minutes are taken and hours wasted!

- Anonymous

You really do have to wonder how managers get anything done, with half their time spent in meetings and the other half spent preparing for those meetings.

But the fact is that meetings are how managers get things done. The value of whatever is accomplished is obviously more than the cost of holding that meeting.

Yet almost everyone thinks that meetings with agenda items are a waste of time.

They may be right. A recent nationwide study concludes that the average employee spends about 8.5 hours each week in meetings—nearly two hours a day! Impossible? Take a look.

There are face-to-face meetings, "virtual" meetings, and teleconferences. There are meetings with production, sales, boards of directors, and staff on a regular basis. There are awards presentations when things go well and face-the-music meetings when they don't. And of course, there are all the meetings in-between that people call to protect their turf, gossip, shift responsibility to others, play games, or stroke their own egos.

If You Can't Name It, Eliminate It

Clearly, meetings are expensive. So are they necessary? Some are; some aren't. One way to tell the difference is to name your meetings. If you can't name it, eliminate it.

Business meetings are—or should be—held in order to move effort closer to results. It follows that they ought to be organized around a particular purpose rather than a list of people. Naming your meeting immediately conveys the tone, agenda, and desired result of a particular meeting. It allows you to justify uninviting those who feel entitled to attend the meeting. And it gives those who have better things to do the opportunity to decline or choose an alternate means of involvement, such as receiving a copy of the meeting notes or talking points.

If you must have a face-to-face meeting—the most expensive kind—it ought to be able to fit into one of these six types.

1. Decision
2. Update
3. Recognition
4. Fact-finding
5. Training and Development
6. Clear the air

1. Decision

A decision meeting is a meeting that can't end without a decision. "I'll get back to you" or "let me think about that" are not acceptable closing remarks. Drawing a line in the sand is a powerful motivator. Once people know ahead of time that they will be required to arrive at a decision on a specific issue and will be accountable for that decision, they are more likely to come prepared.

Make sure that your team understands that a decision meeting means that homework must be done before—not during—the meeting. If people are unprepared, they need to be challenged immediately on the importance of the agenda. Then you will either reschedule the meeting or move ahead without them. You can't afford to waste precious time— your own and others'—in decision meetings where people are not prepared to make a decision.

2. Update

An update meeting is a reality check—no good news, no bad news…just information on what's happening. This meeting is designed to filter out emotions and opinions. It's not about where your organization should or could be, but about where you are in regards to achieving goals, managing projects, dealing with conditions, and fiscal responsibility.

Almost by definition, an "update" suggests ongoing progress with an anticipated lack of completion. This has the unfortunate side effect of encouraging people under pressure to sugarcoat the information they provide, in an attempt to appear to be accomplishing more than they are. This helps no one.

An effective leader creates a safe environment for updates. The goal is to encourage people to point out challenges and misinformation, without fear of retaliation or ridicule. Why? Because everyone needs a time and place where they know its okay to point out the elephants in the room— the challenges, misinformation, and fears that are on everyone's mind, but are not being acknowledged. The goal is to identify the elephants openly in order to neutralize their negative effects. Recognition of issues or excuses is a vital step toward resolving them. For this very reason, the leader must resist the temptation to solve peoples' problems at an update meeting.

3. Recognition

The recognition meeting rewards and appreciates. Whenever possible, this should be an event meeting where you hand out awards and detail accomplishments. Have the paparazzi on hand to take pictures for the next company newsletter.

Whether public or private, recognition is motivation. The difference between the two is that public recognition handled appropriately has the added value of motivating others as well.

Since you are generally dealing with competitive people, try establishing a "badge of honor" to be worn or displayed by the recipient during the event or for a specified period of time. Every Monday during football season, my old coach handed out the Purple Pants award to the top lineman. The award actually was a pair of purple uniform pants that the recipient was expected to wear with pride during practice the rest of the week. All week long, everyone on the field and in the bleachers knew exactly which lineman had done the best job in the previous game. It became a matter of honor among us that no one would wear the purple pants two weeks running.

4. Fact-Finding

The objective of a fact-finding meeting is to arrive at an accurate performance assessment. This is when you really do want to let facts get in the way of a good story. The tone should eliminate opportunities for people to manipulate how others see their performances with anecdotes and personal appeal.

Any worthwhile assessment must be based on a set of clearly defined expectations against which measurable results are compared. For this reason, fact-finding meetings are effective only when they are restricted to a review and discussion of hard evidence—not a person's approach, feelings, or intentions.

5. Training and Development

If you plan to conduct your own training meetings, here are a few things to keep in mind: Get people started with "pre-work" on the topic before the session. This can be as simple as asking them to think about the problems they face. Most people don't come to training to learn anything new, but to justify what they're already doing. Get their minds open beforehand so they're ready to be trained.

- Agree on ground rules for the session, and do your housekeeping up front. Put the agenda on the wall or keep it on a screen where everyone can see it. Encourage them not to resist the information, but to ask questions if they disagree with a point you make.

- Involve the trainees by putting them into groups to apply each aspect of the training. Going through the motions sometimes makes things click. Each group will need a spokesperson and a separate scribe to record results of their activities and discussions on flip-chart paper.

THE INCH PRINCIPLE ■ 21 MILLION DOLLAR INCHES OF MANAGEMENT

• Be free with recognition when anyone participates.

• Make sure everyone takes some action at the end of the session. Have each person write a "note to self." This is a reminder—a promise, really—to apply the newly learned skill in a specific way.

6. Clear the Air

A clear the air meeting is designed to get personal drama or conflict out into the open. Like the update meeting, it needs to take place in a safe zone.

Of course, the obvious cathartic benefit of a clear-the-air meeting is that everyone dials back their emotions and refocuses on the work at hand. Since this type of meeting usually involves two parties or factions in disagreement, the leader must once again resist the temptation to choose sides and solve the problem. Your job is to convince both sides to leave their anger, ego, excuses, and list of hurt feelings at the door, and to call out any infractions of this policy. The tone is mediation, where all participants know they will be able to get their feelings out on the table; the objective is to find a solution that works for everyone.

Meetings are a necessary part of business life. Make a point to keep your meetings on track by defining them ahead of time, and you'll have action, accountability, and application.

Name that Meeting

According to one nationwide survey, badly run meetings waste $100 million each year, just in the salaries of those attending. Most managers and executives can confirm this fact. Their hands are tied, and many would say that even their own meetings are a waste of time!

Yet just as haphazard meetings have an untold cost in time and money, effective meetings put millions in an organization's pockets. It's where brilliant strategies are hammered out and innovative ideas are brought to light.

So treat meetings as a cost, and the objective of each meeting as a benefit. A culture of results versus activity will often yield a successful end. The simple practice of naming a meeting according to its objective will eliminate unnecessary meetings, and streamline the ones that are left.

MILLION DOLLAR INCH

#21

Control the Schedule, Maximize Profits, and Enjoy Life

This is the beginning of a new day. God has given me this day to use as I will. I can waste it or use it for good. What I do today is important, because I am exchanging a day of my life for it. When tomorrow comes, this day will be gone forever, leaving in its place something that I have traded for it. I want it to be gain, not loss; good not evil; success not failure; in order that I shall not regret the price I paid for it.

- Author Unknown

magine you had a bank that credited your account each morning with $86,400. The account carried no balance from day to day, and allowed you to keep no cash in your account. Every morning, any unused funds from the day before would be canceled. What would you do? Draw out every cent, of course!

Well, you have just such a bank, and its name is Time. Every morning it credits you with 86,400 seconds. Every night it writes off as a loss any seconds you have failed to invest to good purpose. It carries no balances. It allows no overdrafts. Each night it closes the records of the passing day. Each day it opens a new account. If you fail to use the day's deposit, the loss is yours.

There is no going back. There is no drawing against tomorrow. You can only live in the present—on today's deposit. Invest it wisely on health, happiness, and success.

Businesses are entrusted with time too. There are consequences when they waste time and money in low pay-off activities, work on the wrong end of problems, ignore warning signs, and try to do too much by themselves. The harder managers work, the further behind they fall— that "hamster-on-a-treadmill" feeling. The result of this overwork is a manager and a team that make poor choices that distract from the primary goals. When the tail wags the dog, the manager has lost control.

Whether the goal is to improve efficiency or be more effective, management and the team must stand back and assess where the time is being invested, and whether it is being invested wisely. The key is to assess activities and demands in light of what is really important to success.

Time is your most precious resource. It is perishable, it is irreplaceable, and it can't be saved up. It can only be reallocated from activities of lower value to activities of higher value. The very act of taking time to assess your time before you spend it will begin to improve your ability to control your schedule immediately.

Controlling the schedule begins with the individual. It starts with clearly defining high payoff activities. It requires that you determine your priorities—those things that you and your team must do on a consistent basis to achieve the goals you set. And you are wise to consider where a person is most productive, given her natural talent and energy.

Traditional time management holds that working in your business pushes out working on your business. This means that managers will focus on a demanding activity in exchange for a high-payoff activity where gratification is not immediate. It's hard to differentiate sometimes, though, in a world where technology has trained us that every text, e-mail, and phone call is urgent and important.

If you're not careful, you'll find yourself falling down a rabbit hole in pursuit of low-payoff activities that are demanding, but are also a waste of time, energy, and resources.

We recently had a client who received two urgent-and-important/needs-immediate-attention e-mails on the same day. The first was from accounting; they could not determine which clients were to be billed for $250,000 worth of materials and they needed to get the invoices out that day. The second "urgent" e-mail came from maintenance. A window, it seems, had been left open in the training room, and he had to shut it.

The result of a demanding wild goose chase is that it tends to cause us to ignore preventive maintenance needs such as planning, training, personal development, health, coaching, savings, and fortifying our critical relationships.

THE INCH PRINCIPLE ▤ 21 MILLION DOLLAR INCHES OF MANAGEMENT

You know by now that continually keeping your schedule under control is critical.

Start By Asking Yourself Two Key Questions

1. Should this activity be demanding my attention? Any time you find yourself with too much to do and too little time, ask yourself this question.

2. Is this a good return on the investment of my time? Pursue it only if it adds value to the plan, and allows for growth and development.

Together, these questions help you answer the ultimate question: What is the most valuable use of my time?

Since only one thing can be done at a time, you must constantly organize yourself and your team to be doing the most important thing at every moment. This process enables you to choose what to do first, what to do second, what to delegate, and what not to do at all. It provides a way to organize every aspect of the schedule so that your team can succeed.

So you've asked yourself what the most valuable use of your time is. Here's how to know if you've answered it. Watch for...

1. Neither Demanding nor High Return

These activities are a liability to success. Color these **RED** for *stop*. Remove the albatross from your list, or ignore it and let it die a slow, natural death. You'll need authority to pull the plug; if you don't have it, get it from the appropriate person. Report any time abuses without anger, frustration, complaints, righteous indignation, or criticism until you have permission to leave the activity behind.

2. Demanding But Offer a Low Return

These activities need leadership. The demand is generally established by other people, so dealing with them is an endlessly reactive process. You'll spend too much time spinning your wheels in that process, so color these **YELLOW**—*proceed with caution.* Take responsibility to baby sit these demands only until the responsible party is identified and a clean hand-off is made.

3. Demanding and High Return

We should b heavily vested in these "highly productive" activities. Paint them **GREEN** for *go for it.* Going green means being assertive—controlling your own schedule, focusing your energy, and staying on the tasks at hand. The results will speak for themselves.

4. High Return but Not Demanding

These activities will usually pay off big in the future, so they need to be scheduled now. Many managers take better care of the lawn than they do their own health, finances, and long-range business objectives. These activities do not become a priority until someone is at the door to collect. Color these activities **BLUE** *for opportunity.* Investing time and energy in blue pursuits is an indicator of commitment. You must put preparation on the schedule. Every minute you invest in planning, training, and self-improving saves you twenty minutes in getting the job done.

Control the Schedule, Maximize Profits, and Enjoy Life

Strong management requires a strategy for allocating time—a precious, non-renewable resource you must use wisely to succeed in business.

The first question to ask is, "What is the most valuable use of my time?" Consider goals, priorities, energy, and talent. Then color-code activities in order to create a common language with everyone on the team. Look to delete red, delegate yellow, go green, and schedule blue. You'll enjoy life and maximize profits when you put less-demanding issues where they belong, avoid traditional time-wasters, and stop worrying about things that can't be controlled.

MILLION DOLLAR INCH

Conclusion

Sometimes the hardest part of the journey is believing you're worthy of the trip.

- Glenn Beck

We trust you find the information contained on these pages of *The Inch Principle: 21 Million Dollar Inches of Management* useful for your business situation. Our goal is to open your eyes to the many opportunities around you to manage more effectively. We feel strongly that applying slight adjustments to your management role, as suggested in this book, will make a major difference in all of your management interactions.

If you have found the information useful, make it part of your management education. Consider implementing one or more of the Million Dollar Inches into your current situation. Pass the information to others, so they can benefit as well.

Finally, when we add a few of these inches to our professional life, not only does our work produce positive outcomes, but so does our personal life. For when all is said and done, it's really total life management that results in effectiveness in our careers. Perhaps, then, we can all feel fulfillment of knowing we make a difference.

Indeed, we resonate with the words of Deepak Chopra: "*To have passion, to have a dream, to have a purpose in life. And there are three components to that purpose, one is to find out who you really are, to discover God, the second is to serve other human beings, because we are here to do that and the third is to express your unique talents and when you are expressing your unique talents you lose track of time.*"

Appendix

About the Cornerstones Management Institute

The Cornerstones Management Institute™ (CMI) was founded by John T. Condry and Paul E. Carpenter. CMI is a management training and consulting firm specializing in helping organizations manage drama in the workplace and increase bottom line results.

CMI's flagship program is "Managing in the Zone™," the future of management training and development. It combines education and performance solutions. The Managing in the Zone™ process is a unique management approach that restores the balance of power in today's technology-based workplace and improves productivity and performance. The program combines a common language introduction, online education, day-to-day application, coaching, and a visual management dashboard to improve accountability, communication and decision making.

CMI has a consortium of talented experts in the fields of management, business development, customer development and retention, communication, and human dynamics. CMI's clients come from a wide range of industries, including textile rental, finance, computer technology, retail sales, health care, advertising, automotive industry, manufacturing, engineering, architecture, accounting, telecommunications, and the trade industry. The programs have been customized to fit management challenges in corporate settings, union environment, small business, non-profit and retail operations, as well as entrepreneurs.

Meet John T. Condry and Paul E. Carpenter; The Principals at CMI

John is a popular management development expert, trainer, consultant, speaker, and founder of Career Success Seminars, Inc. He is the author of the highly successful "Cornerstones of Management" training series. His programs include the "Twelve Cornerstones of Managing for High Performance," "Seven Cornerstones of Customer Retention," "Competitive Growth Strategies for Managers," "Negotiating Successful Outcomes for Managers," "Maximum Results Plus." and "Creating a Corporate and Personal Business Leader Vision."

Paul is a management development expert, trainer, consultant, speaker, technology guru, and president of The Non-Traditional Revenue Group (NTR), LLC. The NTR Group was founded in 2001 as a consulting firm with expertise in developing new revenue streams for companies through training and marketing promotion throughout the United States.

For more information about workshops, site licenses, and consulting services, please contact us at info@cornerstonesonline.com.

THE INCH PRINCIPLE ▦ 21 MILLION DOLLAR INCHES OF MANAGEMENT